BEYOND  COPING

FED UP AND NOT GOING TO TAKE IT ANYMORE!

BOB GLINER

ADVOCATE HOUSE

For further information write or call:

Advocate House

P.O. Box 731

Ben Lomond, CA 95005

(408) 338-3354

Cover Design by John Blanchard

Library of Congress 82-090716

ISBN: 0-910029-01-6

Printed in the United States of America

0   9   8   7   6   5   4   3   2

To Sylvia Gliner
who helped point the way

"When it comes to social change, Bob Gliner is a one-man movement."

Linda Goldston, *San Jose Mercury-News*

TABLE OF CONTENTS

Part II — Beyond Coping: Dealing with Our Problems

Coping in America:
An Overview

1

Jim Johnson, a thirty-five year old engineer, comes home from his job at Lockheed, hurriedly eats dinner with his wife and two kids, then settles down in front of their new color television for an evening of *Quincy, Love Boat, Laverne and Shirley,* and *Store Detective.* Three hours later his wife announces it's time to go to bed, turns off the set, and they follow each other upstairs. The next night he will watch the Raiders/Vikings game, and a re-run of *Mission Impossible.*

The Samuelsons, with a combined income of $45,000, sell their three bedroom, two bath split level for $100,000, making a profit of $30,000 over what they paid for it, and move into a $150,000 four bedroom, three bath in a better part of town. Their monthly payments will be $1100 for thirty years. In addition, they order $5,000 in new furnishings to match their recently acquired residence. Next summer they are thinking of buying a camper in order to take a two week vacation in Yellowstone.

After three years of individual therapy, twenty-seven

year old Sally Martin, lonely and unable to meet anyone she can really relate to, enrolls in EST. A short time later she purchases a book on T.A., **I'm Okay, You're Okay,** and **I Ain't Much Baby, But I'm All I've Got.** After the EST training is over, and she has read the books, she joins an encounter group.

Mary Benton and Paul Hershey, students at a large midwestern university, pause briefly on their way from their dorm rooms to class to get stoned. It is a daily ritual for Mary and Paul. Later, in class, they giggle over a remark their English professor has made, then become deeply engrossed in the doodles Mary draws on the top of her desk.

What do Mary, Paul, Sally, Jim and the Samuelsons have in common? They are *coping;* that is, they are engaged in a lifestyle which enables them to feel comfortable while at the same time avoiding problems which directly confront them. Coping isn't new. People throughout recorded history have always had ways of coping with situations they couldn't face, with problems that seemed beyond their control. Yet, such coping behavior was usually reserved for a small segment of the population, a group under attack or persecution for their political or religious views, and then only for brief periods of time. Similarly, in the United States today, poor people and nonwhite minorities often use alcohol and drugs as ways of coping with problems they face in the context of a largely indifferent and hostile white middle class majority. What is especially significant about the coping behavior going on in American society, however, is that not only are poor and nonwhite persons engaged in such behavior, but it has become the dominant lifestyle for the vast majority of Americans. Coping exists:

- when the city of San Francisco asks for federal aid of 1.4 million dollars to beef up their police force in order to deal with the rising crime rate, rather than address the causes of crime and attempt to fund programs which will root out these causes;

- when a welfare caseworker spends her nine hour work day checking on the eligibility requirements of her clients rather than organizing them to lobby for programs which will guarantee them a decent standard of living;

- when millions of Americans spend the vast majority of their free time as spectators vicariously watching professional athletes live out on the football field the competition and excitement they wish could be a part of their day-to-day lives;

- when up to a third of all high school students on the West Coast regularly cut class or stay away from school all together, rather than confront the boring and irrelevant educational institutions they have been mandated to attend;

- when millions of middle class women spend each Saturday at the nearest shopping mall purchasing clothes and cosmetics in order

3

to make them more "beautiful", rather than dealing with and questioning where the definition of "beautiful" comes from and the status of women in general in American society;

- when 50 percent of the outpatients at Kaiser Hospital reveal they are seeking *medical* assistance for *emotional* problems;
- when an unemployed worker takes a job unrelated to his interests, rather than organize other unemployed workers to lobby for better jobs;
- when someone joins the military to avoid making decisions about their life;
- when an academic sociologist limits her research to those areas which easily translate into statistical significance, rather than address the real problems facing American society and becoming involved in helping to solve these problems;
- when an assembly line worker regularly gets high in order to deal with the day-to-day monotony of his job, rather than joining with other workers in urging their union to press for quality of work improvements;
- when someone spends night after night at a singles bar even though they have never found anyone there to relate to;
- when a middle aged couple spend an entire

year planning for a trip to Europe as a way of solving their marriage problems;

- when an engineer lavishes half his salary on monthly payments for his new Porsche as a means of attracting a women who will love him;

- when we vote every four years for a Reagan or a Carter because they're the only official names on the ballot, rather than because either candidate actually represents our interests.

Why do most Americans use coping mechanisms to negotiate their way through an average day? Why do we find it so difficult to confront and deal with our problems? On the surface, the most apparent reason seems to be that we don't know how to do otherwise. In fact, most of us do not view coping as an escape at all, but rather see it as the only acceptable and normal way of facing up to those things that bother us.

Coping, for most of us, is as American as apple pie. Very early in life we are socialized into the proper way of dealing with situations that make us uncomfortable. Through television ads, situation comedies, our public school system, and our parents we quickly learn that there are two types of problems in our world: personal problems, meaning those issues which we must deal with; and social problems, those things that others — the larger society — will deal with, and which need not concern us. Personal problems, for children, are quickly defined as doing one's homework, finding friends to play with, getting a place on the Little League team and not having to go see Grandma this weekend. Social problems, on the other hand, are those things which are on the front page of the newspaper — issues which the President or Congress or the police or fire department will deal with.

Our public schools do their best to make sure that social problems are always seen as "out there" — issues we need not think about. The three R's are the mainspring of elementary education, taking up by far the vast majority of a child's time in school. The period left over is divided between learning something about the physical sciences, health, physical education, and social studies. No problems whatsoever are associated with the content of the material involved in learning the three R's. Nor do school children learn to associate social problems with learning about science, health, or running about the playground. The one area of study ostensibly bearing some resemblance to social problems is social studies, but even when this discipline is taught, it largely comes out spelled **history**, an area of study the child can do nothing about, since what is history has already happened.

Scant attention is paid to problems a child might face in his or her immediate social environment; rather, it is assumed that the Pilgrims or Columbus or the names of the states are of burning interest to every elementary school student. As a result, elementary school students have little idea how to solve social problems they may be faced with and have to adapt other mechanisms for dealing with those situations when they directly confront them. Yet, many elementary students have little to worry about, since they will never have to directly deal with social problems at all. This is because the schools do not teach children how to define social problems, or relate personal troubles to social issues; rather, emphasis is taken away from the *social* world of the child, and placed on his or her *individual* success.

The public schools are not alone in getting children to define problems in strictly personal terms and in ways that can do little to affect the course of the surrounding community or society. Television shows, particularly family situation comedies, reinforce the public school effort by depicting the major crises of life as stealing pies out of the refrigerator when mother's not looking, or borrowing dad's car. Children are also exposed to the proliferation of crime shows, but the lesson that is conveyed here is not that children should get involved in solving the causes of crime, but rather that if one commits a crime, no matter how exciting or well thought out, he or she shouldn't get caught. At the same time, the child learns that social problems such as crime are easily handled by a wide variety of professionals, and consequently it is a problem he need not concern himself with. Nowhere on television are there community organizers helping poor people lobby for a change in government priorities, or labor leaders organizing strikes around occupational alienation, or students organizing to change the curriculum of their schools.

Parents do not offer much better role models when it comes to confronting and solving problems in their world. Most parents do not conceptualize their personal problems as related to social causes, nor if they do, do they know what to do about them. Parents, like their offspring, often have little understanding of the troubles they experience, and so, unused to solving problems on their own, become only too willing to take those solutions offered by others, cures which, more often than not, result in coping, rather than treatment.

If our public schools, t.v. shows, and parents do not teach children about social problems or how to deal with them, they do provide good examples of coping behavior for children to imitate. If dad has a hard week at the office, then what better way to face up to the issue than to buy a couple of six-packs and spend the weekend in front of the t.v. set watching three or four football games? If mom is bored or frustrated by being stuck home with the kids all week, or working full time and taking care of the kids and house during the remaining hours, then what better way for her to deal with her problem than by going out and buying a new dress? T.v. also helps crystallize for children commercial solutions to often noncommercial problems. The way to attract men is to drink diet Pepsi; if he kissed you once, will he kiss you again? be certain, try Certs; a water bed from the Bedroom saved our relationship.

II

One of the things that makes coping so attractive as a lifestyle is that it is safe. Coping is a way of trying to solve a problem without having to risk anything or put

8

anything on the line. Since coping does not get at the root causes of our problems, we never have to worry that the particular coping behavior we are engaged in will ever substantially alter the social order. From the political perspective of those in power, this is advantageous. If individuals are preoccupied with coping behavior as "solutions" to their problems, then they have little time or energy left over to change a political-economic system which might have given rise to these problems in the first place. In the same sense, by stressing individual solutions to problems that are social in nature, coping insures that most of us will be isolated and powerless, unwilling and unable to define our problems as social in origin and equally resistant to organizing collectively.

The problems most of us face are not, however, simply individual problems which we can take a pill, purchase a new car, buy a new sport coat, go to a football game, or undergo intensive psychotherapy to eliminate. Rather, our personal problems are deeply embedded in the social structure and value framework of American society. Take, for example, the constant anxiety and stress most of us feel from a day at the office, and the ride home on a crowded freeway.

The way many Americans define this problem is by trying to figure out where *they* went wrong. What is it about *their* personal attitude and conception of the world that might be causing them to feel this way? The solution, then, is to either change how they feel about traffic jams and work, switch occupations, take two or three Valium before going to the office, or engage in more physical exercise after they get home.

Another interpretation of the stress and anxiety most of us feel, however, is that it is generated by the very traffic and job conditions in which we find ourselves. Consequently, stress and anxiety cannot be alleviated until traffic and job conditions change, a transformation which can only be brought about by organizing collectively with others, a task few of us are prepared to undertake.

The issue is even more complex, however, for work itself is tied to other segments of society. Part of the reason why so many Americans feel uneasy about the hours spent at the office or factory is that they have little to show for their efforts and can take little pride from the hodge-podge of items which the corporations that engage their labor disseminate to the larger population. Yet, they must continue to produce such items for this is where the jobs are. Further, they must take their paycheck and go out and buy the very goods they are producing. If they do not, the corporations that employ them will cease making profits, they will be laid off, and eventually the economy will collapse. **Yet, the economic system insures that items will continue to be purchased by offering them up as a way of coping with the very alienation work conditions generate.** If I cannot take pride in my job, then I can, at the very least, take the benefits I receive and go out and purchase a meaningful identity elsewhere. In fact, this is exactly what I have been taught to do. And the more items I purchase, ostensibly the more job security I will feel. Coping, then, becomes a way of insuring corporate profits. To transform the conditions which lead to worker alienation, stress and uneasiness, means to transform the entire economy. Therefore, we cannot cease our coping lifestyle unless we also want to lose our jobs.

Coping is good for business in other ways. Not only do many of us find little of worth in our jobs, a problem even more prevalent among younger workers raised on the expectation that they will find meaningful employment, but few other institutions exist to compensate us for our efforts. For example, organized religion is on the decline; we have never been a particularly political people; and few of us are imbued with a lifelong search for truth and knowledge. Consumerism is a way of dealing with this problem. Another is putting all our energy into our inter-personal relationships, an orientation which puts a lot of pressure on these relationships to succeed.

To make sure that we don't fail, we buy those material products necessary for "success" — the right deodorant, the right sweater, the right cosmetic, the right condominium. We also begin to purchase books to find out how to better communicate, enroll in encounter groups to find out how to better relate, and take vacations at "in" resorts. Unfortunately, most of us attempt to set up the best of all possible living together arrangements without changing any other aspect of our lives which might have some bearing on our ability to find happiness. We assume that we can be honest and open, feel sensitive and loving with our mate while working at stress- and anxiety-provoking jobs, spending hours on crowded freeways, and worrying about whether anyone else is infringing on our property. Our property, in fact, our relationship, and the house that surrounds it, becomes most important now, because that is all we have left; it is what we are, and we guard it most jealously.

If our property, wife or husband, color t.v., car, kids, is all that we have left, it means that we cannot share them with others, for then, we would be nothing (no thing). It also means that each of us remains isolated from each other, separated by our possessions and our desire to self-actualize, to cope in our own individual way. From the perspective of corporate America, it means that each of us must have his *own* swimming pool, power mower, massage table, body lotion, garbage compactor, table saw and all of the other accouterments that go into making a good relationship.

As our inability to confront elements of stress at work has us turn to consumerism and intimate relationships for compensation, so too, our inability to find marital happiness in a world in which we are powerless leads us to consult marriage counselors and a variety of therapists to find out how to cope. Yet, do such counselors advise us to examine our lives in the context of American society? Hardly. When we are asked to try and understand ourselves, it is in relationship to how our parents brought us up or how our wife or husband relates to us.

For a therapist to get us to seek the roots of our marital discord in how our neighborhood is organized, in the political and economic structure and the values which it promulgates, would be to then recommend that we need to transform such a society if we indeed wish to find marital bliss. Therapists aren't trained for such an exercise. So much easier to recommend an individual solution, to urge clients to find intimacy without leaving the context of their own heads, or, at best, without transcending the walls of their family units. The end result, of course, is that many clients, having failed to confront the cause of their marital or personal problem, end up coming back for more of the same, or they may even try a different brand.

Therapy becomes a way of coping with a problem without solving it, insuring constant profits for those on the other side of the couch, draining energies away from those who might, if better counseled, direct their efforts toward more rewarding goals. This is not to say that some therapy is not necessary to deal with acute psychological symptoms, but rather, once the symptoms have been reduced, it is necessary to get at the underlying causes.

The fact that coping has become big business has had other, less than honorable results. If the pressure to succeed in our interpersonal relationships has made us insecure, easy victims for corporate ads and self-help therapies, so too, it has drained the land of natural resources, both the ores and chemicals needed to supply our superfluous consumer appetites, but also the mental energies sapped by having to think up ever more elaborate coping mechanisms: pet rocks, primal screams, backless pants. The more frustrated we become at being unable to deal with our personal problems, the more we seek to blame outside forces — the Russians, the poor, the blacks — the bigger defense and police budget we approve in our names as a way of coping. This defense budget — $220

13

billion — is also helpful when it comes to guaranteeing a steady supply of raw materials from other nations. It is no secret that many of these materials come from nations governed by dictatorships — virtually the entire central and south American continents, for example — whose populations are generally living at the starvation level and who could make much better use of these raw materials than we do. Yet, it is our defense dollars, troops, and military aid which often keep these dictatorships in power.

Unfortunately, it is this same defense budget that leaves us without adequate funds to deal with social ills — crime, drug addiction, alcoholism, poor health, mental illness — coping mechanisms most often used by the poor who are unable to adopt a more acceptable lifestyle. By defining poverty as being unrelated to other political and economic priorities, we insure that the problem will never be solved and that the poor will have to continue to cope in ways the rest of us find illegal, abhorrent, or immoral.

We also insure that what little money is spent on crime prevention, drug abuse, and state mental hospitals will be money that is misspent, since it does not go to programs designed to get at the root cause of the issue. We will, however, be able to guarantee steady employment for social workers, police, prison guards, and psychiatric technicians as the more affluent members of American society seek to cope with those who might otherwise threaten their "security".

III

The following pages are an attempt to describe the coping lifestyles many Americans engage in, as well as the implications of these coping lifestyles for American society. As coping is a problem not only for those who fall prey to its excesses, but for those affected by the coping lifestyles *others* engage in as well, we will attempt to describe in the second part of this book how we might stop coping and begin confronting the problems which plague us.

PART I

Educating the Victim: How Schools Teach Coping

2

Perhaps the first place we learn to use coping behavior is in our elementary school classrooms. Here, we are suddenly faced with the realization that somehow there's a difference between what happens in the classroom, and the experiences we have once we leave the school grounds; and that there is little we can do to bridge this gap. It's not that learning about Indians and fractions and geography isn't interesting, it's that the manner in which we learn about these things differs considerably from the way we learn things on the "outside".

In school, subjects are divided up into specific time periods. We typically spend the morning telling ourselves that we must think about math at 8:30, reading at 9:30, and writing at 10:30. This is followed by a lunch period, after which we train our cranial capacities on an hour of physical science, and an hour of social studies.

Not only is the manner in which we learn subjects fragmented into specific time blocks, but the subjects themselves are seldom taught in a way which relates each

16

to the others. When we are reading, it is presumed that this is all we can do. We cannot read and do social studies; we cannot read about the Civil War. When we are writing, emphasis is on spelling and use of grammar, not *at the same time* on a discussion of a problem we had with our older brother or sister. In math, we only add or subtract, the numbers themselves do not refer to anything concrete like: you've got five minutes to do the dishes if you expect to be able to watch your favorite t.v. show; how long would it have taken you if there wasn't any television in the house?

The one subject that is supposed to relate to what's happening to us in our "real lives", social studies, is largely spent discussing history, and then, typically, *ancient* history, not important things which may have happened yesterday or last week or even during the last decade. Social studies curriculums also ask us to focus our attention on specific topics each year. For example, in the third grade we are supposed to have a burning desire to investigate the Mayflower, and then in the fourth grade, South America heads our interest list, and in the fifth it will be California. Yet, how many third graders pass their time outside the classroom engrossed in problems experienced by the Pilgrim fathers? In the same way, how many fourth grade kids divide the way in which they conceptualize the world into spelling, reading, writing, arithmetic, physical science and social studies? No one experiences the world in this fashion. When a child encounters a problem, he doesn't attempt to compartmentalize it; rather, he attempts to solve it in an *interdisciplinary* manner,

17

applying *everything* he knows. How then is our average elementary school student to make sense out of these two different realities? He isn't. Rather, he quickly learns that there is one reality for the school he attends, and another for the playground and after school activities he engages in. Yet, why doesn't he make an attempt to bridge the gap between these two worlds of knowledge? Because he doesn't know how. Another look at the social studies curriculum may shed some light on why.

Social studies does far more than attempt to educate students about world history or the "peoples of other lands". It also attempts to convey the message that the child lives in a problem-free society, or, if there have been problems in the past, they have long since been solved so there is nothing much to worry about. Since history is emphasized, social problems currently facing American society are rarely, if ever, discussed. Nor, for that matter, are the everyday personal problems most students deal with in their families and in their neighborhoods. And, in the exceptional instance when these topics are broached, never are possible methods for solving these problems brought up. For the child whose father has just lost his job, watched his parents go through a marital separation, tried to breathe smog-filled air after an hour's soccer game, had his toys ruined by the kid down the street, or had his favorite television show interrupted by a news-break picturing police attempting to control an angry crowd protesting the rising price of food, such a curricular oversight has startling effects. Either the problems he experiences or watches on television are not real, or, are

18

not important — since the teacher never talks about them — or, they are important and it is the school curriculum which is meaningless because it does not mention them.

But equally crucial, the fact that these topics are not discussed and that solutions and possible ways of bringing these solutions about are not mentioned, means that the child is ill-equipped to confront problems he must eventually deal with. Unable to gain an understanding of such problems in the classroom, and having little idea how to go about solving these problems, the child is forced to *cope* with situations he might otherwise be able to confront and effectively deal with. At the same time, his inability to face up to and solve problems on the "outside" makes it impossible for him to solve problems on the inside, in the classroom curriculum. How can a child tell his teacher that he doesn't understand the relationship between his father's alcoholism and the math problem she wants him to do? How is the child to bridge the gap between the names his classmates call him because he is not as fast as they are, and a discussion of the Pilgrims, when no one tells him that such a connection is important and no one shows him how to make it?

Torn between two sets of legitimate subject matter, two sets of "curricular" demands, the child quickly becomes powerless, unable to understand how to solve problems in his home, on his block, or in his community, and unable to make sense out of the fragmented forms of knowledge bestowed on him at school. Nor is he able to know how to correct the situation. For some children, the best way of coping with this intolerable discrepancy is

19

to attempt to ignore both worlds, and instead, become involved in sports, television, or fanciful daydreams about a world which will someday make sense, when one grows up to be a real doctor, lawyer, or Indian chief.

Elementary education, then, sets a precedent which will follow a child throughout his life, by attempting to show him what is important and what is not, and by failing to teach him how to deal with personal and social problems which people his world.

Part of the reason why elementary schools do not teach problem solving is because the larger society has never expected them to do so. Schools exist according to both parental and school board conceptualizations, to educate students into the dominant values of American society and to teach students basic skills so that they can survive. Among the values emphasized are competition and individualism. A student learns individualism by working on his own and the curriculum is designed in such a way as to prevent group problem solving and cooperation as a learning experience, thereby insuring that all students can in fact do is try to solve problems by themselves. Competitive grading also guarantees that there will be winners and losers and that cooperation is not possible. What such educational values mean as well is that students, isolated and alone in their individual learning cocoons, will be powerless to affect educational problems they may now be faced with, and equally powerless to confront problems they will face later on because they do not understand how to organize collectively, or even why they might need to do so.

Schools also have a priority to teach basic skills, for which social problem solving does not qualify. Accordingly, it becomes acceptable to experiment with different ways of teaching the 3 R's more effectively, but not to play around with a social studies curriculum that might call into question sacred values and taboos. Indeed, millions of dollars have been poured into teaching the big three, but scarcely a cent into teaching students how they might apply these in conjunction with a social studies curriculum designed to solve problems in their everyday world. It is also why it is acceptable to teach multicultural education as a course in Chinese or Mexican American cooking, rather than discussing the dynamics of intercultural interaction and racism in American society.

Schools are also reluctant to engage in such curricular matters because parents might complain. What parent wants his child coming home from school demanding to know his rights, since most parents have little understanding of their own. Nor do parents feel children are responsible enough to discuss and try to solve personal and social issues, though these same children may be dramatically affected by these very problems. Since teachers have little understanding of how to solve problems in their own lives, they too do their utmost to shy away from any such subject matter. Schools of education prepare them for this state of ignorance by focusing on everything but a relevant and involving curriculum. Where then is such a curriculum to come from? If parents, teachers, and school board members do not want to bring it about, then how can an eight year old?

In junior high school and high school, the gap between personal experience and what takes place in the classroom widens. While these grade levels continue to talk about classroom education as preparation for the real world of adulthood, most students have long since realized that the reason they are in school is because this is where their parents want them to be, and because this is what one is supposed to do from the ages of 13 to 17. Yet, it is one thing to have one's body seated in a wooden desk six hours a day while the teacher talks about diagramming sentences, the presidency of Andrew Jackson, algebra, and biology. It is quite another to fix one's mind to the blackboard, especially when there are so many other interesting and important things happening outside these rows of chairs. *I wonder if she'll go with me to the party Saturday night? If we beat Eastside, then we might have the city championship. Fonzie's such a fox, God, if I could only . . . Wait till I get that new 350 engine and that job at the Arco. If there are people in outer space and they came down here, wow, what a trip!*

Junior and senior high school curriculum rarely goes further than that of the elementary school when it comes to talking about personal and social problems and what to do about them. While there are a few *elective* classes on social issues in some high schools, most students by this time have already turned off to them, not understanding why they should suddenly be important, or how such a class might relate to their *real* problems which are now defined almost exclusively as personal in character, that is, as only affecting them, and which only they can solve.

Social problems affecting the larger society, since they are not considered important by cops and robbers television shows, parents, or previous experience with curriculum at the elementary school level, and are apparently not related to the life and death problems of dating, mating, car repair, or sports, are obviously neither a necessary nor a crucial part of one's education. Yet, even when such issues classes are offered, they are designed to explore problems, not solve them. Even if a student manages to get enthusiastic about a particular issue discussed in such a class, his enthusiasm rapidly fades as he attempts to integrate the problem he is thinking about and the unrelated experiences he must undergo in his subsequent classes. By the end of the day he has lost the feeling, or it is quickly erased by the interests of friends not enrolled in the class, who want to go for a ride, or pass the ball around, or catch a soap opera, or do their homework. Far easier just to go along, especially when one doesn't know how to do otherwise; when it takes so much energy to pursue the issue, when no one else really cares.

Unable to confront a fragmented, compartmentalized, and meaningless curriculum, students at this level quickly become mental dropouts, daydreaming their way through five or six years of secondary education, like they will later daydream their way through an assembly line or paper-shuffling job. Or, they cope by ignoring what goes on in school, in deference to extracurricular activities they can easily relate to and in which they can find quick and meaningful rewards. While a few students attempt to organize a noon rally or bring in an outside speaker, the fact that such activities must take place outside the domain of the traditional curriculum and are typically one-time-only events makes the message and meaning of these activities crystal clear. They can go on so long as they don't affect the real curriculum, so long as they do not disturb the planned agenda of the school district, so long as they do not take away the power of the teacher and the principal.

Yet, there is really no need to worry, since the average student has no difficulty equating the thousands of hours he must spend in the classroom, to the two he spends per year at noon or after school listening to Tom Hayden tell it like it is — if he attends at all. Accordingly, student government becomes an exercise in setting a date for the senior prom, rather than debating and acting on the right of students to have a say in what curriculum is offered, who is going to teach it, and how it will be taught.

While most students cope with this experience by mentally dropping out and focusing their energies on after school activities, some physically drop out, unable to wait for the bell to ring. Laboring under the illusion that since high school curriculum is irrelevant and boring, therefore it must not be necessary, these students opt for a real world existence of marriage and an eight to five job. *Man, if I could only open up my own motorcycle shop and marry my old lady, wow, that would be real freedom!* Unfortunately, while high school may not prepare a student to confront personal and social problems, it also does not prepare him for marriage and the available job market. Indeed, the inability of high school curriculum to discuss real issues leaves students to nourish the illusion that it is always better on the outside. The physical drop-out, however, soon finds that the freedom he had hoped for is only too easily replaced by the slavery of unemployment or employment in a job which is even less exciting than his high school English class. Nor is marriage, for most, a panacea, as the presence of children, mounting bills and the growing realization that we have settled down too early quickly comes to occupy all our waking moments.

Public attitudes toward high school education do their part to guarantee that students will not take such an educational experience seriously. While students are told they must be in high school in order to be eligible for a job, or in any case, to gain entrance into a college which will prepare them for employment, there is little about high school, or, as we shall see, college education that prepares students for specific vocational tasks. Beyond the goal of vocational education, however, high school is seen by the vast majority of parents as necessary for the development of an educated populace which has a general understanding of knowledge and ideas prevalent today and important in our historical experience. Yet, the very nature of high school curriculum belies the importance of such knowledge, for students are not permitted to practice any of its tenets. The Bill of Rights should only be used when one is not on school grounds. The right of referendum and recall have nothing to do with inept teachers. Protests against our involvement in a foreign war, or in the development of more nuclear weapons are not the business of public school students. Not only are the ideas students might inadvertently learn not considered important by the general public, but students are considered irresponsible if they attempt to express these ideas.

The problem goes deeper, however, because all of the adolescent years are held to lack importance as well, whether we count the time spent on school grounds or somewhere else. The education adolescents experience is not considered significant because it does not focus on ideas society considers important, and in a way that such ideas might prove useful. Therefore, most youth are seen as parasites, making no contribution to the well-being of society, and, as a consequence, having no legitimate status. Moreover, what adolescents do is not to be taken seriously because they do not work, despite the fact that there are no jobs for them and we do not want them to work, anyhow. Since they do not get paid for going to school, and what they do in school is not considered meaningful, we cannot consider education to be their form of employment. Nor can we treat their relationships seriously because they are too young to be really involved, and besides, sexual intimacy is not a part of the school curriculum. Such contradictory messages leave most youth in a Nowhere Land, cut off from making a meaningful contribution to society, without worthwhile roles to play, waiting out their chronological sentence till they are "old enough" to be granted a ticket of admission. With questionable citizenship and lacking the knowledge and motivation to confront the problem head on, youth retreat into their own subcultures to pass the time, to cope with an otherwise worthless existence. Yet, such coping devices are only temporarily effective at best, since their bodies remain in the classroom.

III

If we have been passing our high school years waiting for a chance at the real thing, an education which makes sense and deals with topics and concerns we are truly interested in, then college and university education quickly become a disappointing experience. The freshman and sophomore years at most public universities are spent fulfilling general education requirements, which means, sampling from a broad variety of separate and distinct courses so as to get some notion of different subjects to specialize in later on.

This is little different from high school offerings except that there are a greater variety of courses to choose from and classroom presentations are more sophisticated. When we enter the upper division we are expected to specialize in a course of study which will ultimately lead to some type of employment or make us into better citizens, able to comprehend and participate in the ongoing intellectual and political world. On either count, most college and university curriculums are dismal failures, enabling students to be neither adequately prepared for the jobs they will encounter, nor equipped to participate in intellectual and political life.

Students choosing between a general intellectual understanding and job preparation are usually making a choice between the humanities and arts, on the one hand, and engineering, the sciences, and business on the other. But, no matter, because the narrow educational experience they receive in either "camp" will have a greater impact on their potential experience as "adults" in America than any specific major. The first thing we find is that knowledge, even within the broad categories of business, science, and humanities, has been carved up into miniature fiefdoms, each vying for a larger piece of the intellectual pie. In the social sciences, for example, psychologists and sociologists rarely talk to each other except to point out the fallacies inherent in the other's field. Nor is there any communication between artists and philosophers, or historians and geographers.

Things are not much better on the other side of the campus, as manpower development experts rarely consult with biologists or engineers. One of the results of this kind of specialization and resulting intellectual isolation is that students majoring in any specific discipline graduate with an extremely biased perception of the world. While many of us do take classes outside our major field of specialization, we are left on our own to determine how such classes relate to our primary field of study. What instructor, for example, is likely to discuss the relationship between English literature and sociology? Most of us avoid the problem by minoring in a field closely resembling our major. A sociology student takes anthropology courses, a chemistry major may minor in physics.

Yet, like the outside world the elementary and high school student must deal with, upon graduation, areas of specialization break down; one finds that problems in everyday life are not neatly divided into areas of psychology, business, English, or physics. One is not simply a sociologist one hour, then an historian, then a biologist the next. Rather, the world is interdisciplinary, and each of us must be a bit of all these things in order to effectively deal with our problems. Even within the occupation we choose, issues often reach well beyond our academic specialization. This holds true for those whose academic course work was ostensibly job-oriented — those in business, engineering and the sciences — as well as for those specializing in a more general major. A good engineer must now consider more than the mechanics of building a bridge; he must also take into account the environmental impact such a bridge might have on traffic patterns, and also the pollution caused by cars traveling over its span. Psychotherapists, in order to gain a more accurate perception of their clients' problems, should know something about possible societal causes of their clients' behavior — does a symptom like uncontrollable anxiety result from bureaucratic pressure experienced on the job? Does a child feel the need to rebel at home because she lacks respect for a junior high school education which in her eyes has little relevance for her life? Medical doctors must begin to confront the societal causes of their patients' illnesses as well, especially in the area of cancer and heart disease.

Yet, no need to really worry, because the jobs most college graduates will come to occupy will have little to do with the kind of work an engineer, psychotherapist or medical doctor *should* be engaged in. Rather, persons choosing these occupations or any one of a thousand others will be pigeon-holed and compartmentalized into even greater degrees of specialization than they now experience within their major field of study, and it is such compartmentalization which will make them power-less to affect decision making in the corporations and social service agencies which employ them, unable to understand the larger ramifications of what they are doing, to see the bigger picture. And this is exactly how most public and private corporations want us, because it makes us easier to control. Besides, not everyone can be a leader. For the student who skips the four year college and settles for a two year community college experience aimed even more rigorously at vocational education, the chances of advancement up the corporate hierarchy are still more restrictive, as early specialization hinders general problem-solving ability.

The issue is more complex, however, than the fact that students, educated along compartmentalized lines, are ill prepared for real effectiveness in the world they will encounter when they graduate. Even the way knowledge within a given discipline is conveyed is often at odds with the extracurricular experiential framework of the student. This is particularly true in the social sciences, an area of study encompassing the personal and social problems most students will have to come to terms with at some point in their lives. Students majoring in psychology must choose courses under such glamorous headings as *personality theory, clinical psychology,* or *experimental methodology.* In sociology, the titles might be: *social theory, criminology,* or *modern family.* The difficulty is that we do not use our knowledge passively; when we think about something we do not first consider whether it is part of a social theory, or experimental psychology. Rather, we assemble knowledge in a way which helps us solve a problem. Course titles which might better fit knowledge use might include such headings as: *experiencing and alleviating anxiety, dealing with poverty* or *designing a better environment.* Breaking knowledge into passive divisions or compartments within a field of study makes it all the more difficult for the student to figure out how to integrate such knowledge into daily life, as well as applying it on the job. Yet, most academic disciplines do not consider integration, or practical experience, a valuable form of knowledge, and, as a consequence, leave students to bridge the gap between theory and practice *after* they have graduated. But students no more automatically learn how to make this transition than they automatically learn how to read.

Why aren't university faculty interested in what we do with the knowledge they feed us, or in showing us the relationships between different disciplines, thereby giving us a better perspective of a given issue? A good part of the explanation derives from how faculty conceptualize their role. While the heart of the university is the classroom, faculty are also expected to publish; and in fact, to base their careers and promotions on such publications. This leads to an emphasis on specialization as faculty search for a niche to carve out in their particular fields. As faculty become more and more interested in furthering their careers, they become less and less concerned with what happens in the classroom; as their scholarly status becomes increasingly important, they are less and less willing to entertain any but a discipline-oriented curriculum. A student-oriented curriculum based on real life problems becomes not simply alien, but *unprofessional.* Faculty also become adept at maintaining their territory against encroachment from both faculty within the same discipline, and from challenges by faculty from other disciplines as well. In fact, threats from other disciplines must be avoided at all cost, or one risks having his entire life's work called into question.

As faculty become invested in such issues, they come to feel that *only they* are qualified to teach their area of specialization; only they possess the necessary skills and, more importantly, the credentials, degrees and publications. Mesmerized by career problems, faculty give up control of the university to an administrative elite which comes to substitute bureaucratic priorities for educational excellence or reform. Instead of facilitating the learning process, university administrators come to dominate, deciding how the curriculum is structured, and what new programs will be permitted. The administration, with its bureaucratic tendencies and institutional priorities, then comes to reinforce existing educational compartmentalization and fragmentation.

From this faculty perspective, then, teaching students how to deal with personal and social problems is not only a nuisance, not merely unprofessional, it is unscientific as well. Involvement in problem solving means taking a certain value position, choosing sides. Everyone knows a scientist must be neutral. Besides, what respected journal would publish unscientific material?

And so, there we are, like the curriculum available to us in high school; every so often we chance upon a course that relates to some problem we may be facing. But this experience is soon drowned out in the hundreds of other hours we must spend in courses which have no relationship at all to the problem we are concerned with. Soon it does not matter, for we have already learned to cope, learned to deal with problems in other ways, learned not to expect anything other than what we are getting, and grown to like it that way.

IV

As graduation approaches, we begin thinking about getting a job. The manner with which we approach this subject is indicative of everything the school system has taught us. First, getting a job is *our* responsibility; it has nothing to do with the fact that private and public corporations and government priorities in spending tax dollars may have something to do with the availability of positions. Not only is gaining employment up to us, but only we can solve the getting-a-job problem. After all, we have been raised to think of ourselves as individualists, to compete one on one with others, may the most qualified person win. Yet, on discovering that there are no jobs in our chosen area of expertise, or that four hundred other students are trying for the same "challenging" position, what do we do? Yell out to our compatriots waiting in line to sign up for an interview:

"If we ALL don't get meaningful jobs, then NONE of us will take a job!" Hardly. Rather we say *I'll get by, I've got an aunt who owns a clothing store and she says I can always sell cosmetics, at least until something better comes along.* Or, the truly enterprising among us might say: *"I think maybe I'll go on to graduate school, wait it out, you know, until the situation improves."*

Taking the Job You Never Wanted

3

While, more often than not, high schools, colleges, and universitites do not prepare students for the jobs they will come to occupy on graduation, from another standpoint, twelve or sixteen years of methodical learning has been lesson enough. The occupations the vast majority of students find themselves in are little different from their classroom experience. Instead of asking them to diagram sentences, the task is to mount fenders on a hundred new trucks coming down the assembly line. Instead of asking them to figure out a series of mathematical computations, they must now process several dozen insurance claims. Instead of writing an exam on the four reasons behind U.S. intervention in World War I, they must now come up with a rationale for selling a new kind of dog food or deodorant.

The lack of control students have over their school curriculum is readily transplanted into the powerless occupational positions most now find themselves spending forty hours a week engaged in. The same lack of challenge and meaning follows them to the factory, corporation or social service job. The problem is that many students, particularly those with a college background, had expected their occupational careers to be far different. The realization that they will not be makes their current job situation indeed a bitter pill to swallow. After all, college and university education might have been boring, might have been too fragmented and compartmentalized to make sense, but at least it was only temporary, at least one could keep telling oneself that the four or five or six years was for some greater good, a job that really meant something, that made a difference, that was a contribution others would value.

For those with a scientific, engineering, or business bent, the shattering of illusion comes in the form of having to work on pieces of a project without ever being able to understand or develop a sense of the completed entity. The student of aeronautical engineering now finds himself designing a piece of the wing, with little say in how the overall plane is to be designed, or whether or not a different conception should be used. The chemistry student finds herself working in the lab for a large drug company running tests in an attempt to come up with a more palatable cough syrup, rather than working on new and exotic chemical combinations designed to improve human existence. The business student quickly finds that his road to the top of the corporation is blocked by his lack of contacts with higher executives, and moreover, that he must now compete with hundreds of other middle management personnel for the two or three higher level openings per year. But he cannot stay where he is, because the task he is currently engaged in requires little if any entrepreneurial skill or responsibility.

The student of humanities and social sciences, as we noted in the previous chapter, has a far more difficult time aligning his or her social idealism with the exigencies of the job market. For one thing, there are very few jobs for those wishing to change society, to make communities better places in which to live. For another, those jobs whose ostensible classification might lead students to think they are humanistic in character rarely, if ever, turn out to match the official job description. The person hired as a corrections officer for a prison does not solve the crime problem or rehabilitate inmates; rather, he quickly learns how to run a human warehouse and how to calculate prisoner infractions. The new social worker or eligibility worker hired by a social service agency does not work on solving the problem of poverty, but rather spends the vast majority of her time processing welfare forms and viewing client requests for help as a hassle which must be tolerated. As such, social workers and the persons whose needs they are supposed to administer to become adversaries, enemies negotiating over a five dollar hike in a food stamp allocation.

Yet, millions of sociology, psychology, history, English and philosophy majors will never have to pretend that what they are doing is meaningful because they will never find jobs related to their area of interest; there simply aren't that many positions. Instead, they will find careers as bartenders and cocktail waitresses, postmen, saleswomen, or lower echelon corporate managers with little chance for advancement, or, they will have to content themselves with part time work as itinerant carpenters, craftsmen, waitresses or seasonal help, or they will join the ranks of the unemployed.

Beyond recent high school and college graduates, of course, are those who have long since "come of age", who have already spent ten, twenty, or thirty years in dead-end occupations, offering little relief from performing the same repetitive task over and over, all hope of engagement in a challenging and meaningful experience buried in the corporate ground. How do these millions of workers *cope* with their situation?

II

There are essentially five mechanisms most of us use to cope with a dissatisfying job experience: we can attempt to rationalize our position; we can attempt to change jobs, hoping to find meaning in a new occupation; we can attempt to persuade our company to introduce policies which will make our job more gratifying; we can spend our energies on the fringe benefits of our employment, the paychecks and medical benefits we receive, hoping to find satisfaction off our job; or, we can quit.

The one thing we cannot do, however, is forget about employment, because we need the money in order to survive, and because, regardless of the negative consequences, what defines us as a worthwhile person in

American society is that we can hold down a job. This is especially true for males who are raised to believe that the only way to be a man is to put in a forty-hour work week; increasingly, it is becoming true for women as well, who have come to realize that the only way to real status power is through job and paycheck. Let's take a brief look at each of the coping mechanisms listed above so we can better understand how viable they are in enabling us to deal with our situation.

First, we can justify the hours spent at work by attempting to come up with a rationale for the particular job we are performing An assembly line worker might tell himself that even though it's a drag to have to bolt hundreds of bumpers a day on new cars, the finished product sure looks nice. By seeing the larger product as worth doing, the piece of the product we are working on ostensibly becomes worthwhile also. The problem with this type of rationalization is that it only rings true in the short run — how many times can we keep telling ourselves the same message and have it make up for the hundreds of hours spent in mindless drudgery?

Moreover, many of us have difficulty linking the finished product with the minute task we are engaged in. Nor are many finished products worth identifying with, especially since we have little say in how the product is designed, or what product the corporation we work for is going to manufacture in the first place.

A similar coping strategy results from an attempt to identify with the corporation which employs us. While our individual job may mean very little, General Motors or IBM or U.S. Steel might have a national reputation. Here, however, such a justification can only work when we are not in the plant or at the office. It can only be effective in the eyes of those on the outside — our wives, husbands, friends, children or relatives. Once inside the corporate gates, where everyone has the same status in terms of working for the company, other justifications must be sought.

Another mechanism we use to rationalize our position is by shifting our original goals, changing our expectations of what we want out of a job. For example, we might substitute the security derived from employment in a rigid public bureaucracy for the challenge and meaningfulness of helping humanity. Such feelings of security, we might claim, enable us to focus our attention on activities we are involved in on weekends, or when we come home in the evening. *"I didn't want that kind of responsibility, anyhow, it'd give me ulcers. I'd have to be staying up nights worrying all the time, thinking, did I make the right decision. Supposing it doesn't work? They might fire me."*

A similar approach is to tell ourselves that, after all, work is work, it was never supposed to be meaningful; it's just something we have to do in order to survive. *"And while my job may not be very worthwhile, at least I've got a lot of friends, really a great bunch of gals. And besides, I'm making good money. What more could you ask for?"* Yet, while we may develop good friends at the office, such friendships do not make it any easier to perform the same function day after day — they don't fill

40

out forms, or sell products, or solder thousands of identical wires together. But they do help us relax during lunch and after work at a nearby bar, or on weekends. They do help us to cope.

A second coping mechanism we use is to attempt to change jobs, holding out hope that in another occupation we might find real challenge and excitement. This may be a fantasy we will never act on as we daydream about some moment in the future when the corporation will recognize our talents and we will be promoted. We may, however, go beyond our daydreams and enroll in night school, attempting to learn how to do accounting so we are eligible for transfer out of the warehouse, or we may learn how to become a real estate agent, so we can "go into business for ourselves". Yet, more often than not, promotions, when they come, do not lead to more interesting work, only a temporary respite from the lifelessness one has just emerged from. As soon as we settle into our new task, it too soon takes on the same characteristics as the one we have only recently vacated. Nor is retraining a panacea, for it is often based on the mistaken notion that there are an unlimited number of possibilities out there, if we could but latch on to the right one, if we could just get the right education. In reality there are few challenging jobs available. Like promotion, while re-training may enable us to shift occupational tasks, it does little to give us greater control over the work place, to have a say in fundamental decisions the company will make, to change the manner in which jobs are performed.

A third way in which we cope is by attempting to

41

get high level management to introduce changes in the tasks we perform. Such proposed changes can take a variety of forms. Some call for shifts in the amount of time we must spend doing a specific task. For example, a particularly boring piece of labor may be rotated, so no one person has to spend too long at that task. Job descriptions can also be enlarged so as to include a variety of tasks, thereby giving us a greater sense of accomplishment, and again reducing the amount of time we must spend on one project. Beyond job rotation and enrichment has been the demand for greater decentralization of the work place, and the regrouping of tasks into work teams responsible for either the entire product or a substantial part of the finished commodity. Volvo plants in Sweden are a prime example of this effort, where a group of workers is responsible for assembling an entire engine, and is left to its own devices to decide how this task is to be accomplished.

There are several difficulties with this form of coping. First, are these work alternatives really coping mechanisms by our definition, since they ostensibly address and alleviate a fundamental problem workers experience? Only if they do not deliver what they promise. While making work more interesting in the short run, what happens once we have grown used to our new *set* of jobs? So we only spend two hours a day at each task, rather than the complete eight, how much more meaningful and challenging has each task actually become? Not very. When a plant is decentralized and work teams assemble finished products, if they have little say in what they are to produce or in its design, and moreover, if they do not directly profit from their efforts by sharing in corporate sales, then how much better off are they? Would not the assembling of the same engine week after week be apt to lead to the same boredom, the same lack of excitement and challenge?

Yet, a second reason why most of these efforts to make jobs more tolerable are actually coping mechanisms is because it is the rare worker who initiates these corporate changes, who approaches her foreman or manager with a reorganization plan. Rather, it is the corporation itself and the executives who run it who bring about these alterations. Nor are their efforts based upon sudden humanitarian altruism. No, corporations want to make jobs for their employees more interesting because it's profitable for them to do so. A worker who is satisfied, they reason, will work harder and contribute more, than one who is not.

In actual fact, then, we have no more control over key job decisions that we did before, but what has happened is that we have been co-opted into thinking that we do, that our job is actually more interesting, that management really cares about us and is taking steps to make our occupational lives more interesting. It is also important to emphasize that not all factories are experimenting with alternative organizational plans. This is especially true for persons employed in white collar or middle management positions, whose only claim to meaningful work lies in the "professional" label they may attach to their position. Indeed, paper shufflers have long been ignored in reorganizational plans because it is assumed that because of their status they are not "suffering".

In corporations where management has not encouraged re-organizational changes, why haven't blue collar workers taken the initiative? In order to make this a viable option, we would have to assume that they are not settled into a coping pattern, and that they think an alternative is possible. We would also have to assume that blue collar workers have an overall knowledge of how the plant goes together so that they could conceptualize what such a new design might look like.

Where is this alternative conception to come from? Perhaps from discussions with former colleagues who have made their way up to the corporate hierarchy. But who has worked his way up from the assembly line to foreman to manager to executive? We can think of no one, because the skills gained from assembly line work are not those required of management personnel, whose abilities lie not so much with what they can do with their hands, as with how well they can manipulate people and make decisions. This is why assembly line workers rarely advance beyond shop foremen, and why most middle management personnel start as managers (all our daydreams and stories in **Fortune** magazine to the contrary).

Fragmented into specific job classifications and duties, then, how is the average blue collar worker to formulate an opinion on how a plant should look, especially when she has never been asked, or never considered that it was her place to even put forth such an opinion. Far easier to leave such decisions to others and to not bother thinking about it at all. Nor are unions much

44

help. Used to dealing with bread and butter issues, unions focus their energies on the fringe benefits of employment: higher wages, more job security, better safety in the plant, retirement benefits, hospitalization, longer vacation time. Most workers are as reluctant to approach their shop steward or local union president for a request for quality of work negotiations as they are to approach their supervisor. It just isn't done: just as schools simply do not teach social problems and the tactics of social change. Of course, the vast majority of workers waste little time worrying about these matters; for a job is a job and you do what you can to put up with it.

III

Perhaps the most popular way we have found to cope is through the fringe benefits we receive for our forty hours on the job. A paycheck, besides supplying the basic necessities, enables us to buy a new camper, go on vacation, get a new dress, purchase a new car, or build a shop in our garage. Some corporations provide other benefits to lure the potentially disgruntled worker to sleep. The location of plants is a prime example, with many businesses situating themselves in rolling green hills near where their employees can lead a pleasant life of leisure, that is, when they aren't working. Golf courses and tennis courts have even become standard fare at a few. Yet, regardless of where the corporation or public bureaucracy which employs us is located, most of us pass the hours away, day dreaming off about what we will do once it's five o'clock, or during our two week summer vacation, or what we will buy, or our tennis or basketball game, in much the same way as our high school and college counterparts daydream their way through a formal education which requires their physical, though rarely their mental, participation.

While waiting for the "bell to ring", many of us also pass the time with alcoholic breaks or by getting stoned during lunch. Others of us take uppers or downers, depending on the particular job requirements we are confronted with. And, there are some of us who avoid the whole process as often as possible and call in sick or leave early, no longer able to defer gratification.

Those unable to cope in the fashion described above are left with two possibilities: they must either quit and attempt to find a new job, or they can give up the struggle and join the ranks of the permanently unemployed. Yet, the choice is usually not up to them; rather, in the case of middle management personnel or civil service employees, they are simply laid off for having a "bad attitude", or too many absences. Blue collar workers may be dismissed for failure to keep up with the required piece rate, or the assembly line. Or, corporations may take the entire problem out of our hands, and lay us off regardless of our attitude, because they have decided not to manufacture the particular item we happen to be working on: it is no longer profitable.

Unemployment in American society is a particularly difficult situation to cope with because there is so little we can do about our predicament. As we noted in the previous chapter, responsibility for getting a job lies with us, not those who would employ us. What this means is that we see it as a personal problem which only affects us and which only we can solve. Hat in hand, then, we must go from one factory or corporate employment office or public service bureaucracy to another until we find an opening.

Yet, while it is our responsibility to find a job, *control* over what jobs are available lies with the corporation or with government funding priorities. We, as isolated individuals, are powerless. Yet, not only do unemployed workers have little control over their fortunes, and therefore, in most cases, must accept whatever is offered, but they also suffer in other ways. Many of the fringe benefits they have counted on to justify the days at the office are now no longer available to them. They may have more free time, but they have no one to spend it with. Their friends and neighbors are, in all likelihood, still employed. Their kids are in school. Their wives or husbands are either employed or busy in their own activities. Nor can they go out and spend money, look for a new car, fix up their camper, or add an addition onto the house.

The problem goes deeper because, as we have seen, if our entire identity is based on the fact of employment, then unemployment becomes a shattering psychological experience. How do we identify who we are when a new acquaintance asks: what do you do? No longer do the old rationalizations so well suited for justifying employment in even the most destitute of tasks hold up. For those of us who rationalized rigid bureaucratic and assembly line guidelines as providing a sense of security, being out of work becomes particularly difficult, since all semblance of security has vanished.

Even more shattering, however, is the fact that we must once again assume responsibility over our life, with no bureaucratic rules to help us along, to give us support. We must now, of our own volition, go out and find another job, though dependence on our own abilities does little to conjure up employment where none exists. In a kind of strange and sad way, those of us who came to view our corporation as if it were a protective parent, whose products we identified with despite the discomfort of our own particular position, cannot even indict our former employers for the situation they have placed us in. To do so would leave us with no one to identify with, and no place to look for a job, since we cannot fault the corporate structure and at the same time ask it to give us work. Rather, we must blame ourselves, though there is little we can do about the predicament we now find ourselves in.

IV

Many studies of employee attitudes toward their jobs, whether they be about white or blue collar work, have shown a great deal of job satisfaction. Yet, when the meaning of satisfaction is broken down, it becomes apparent that what most workers are really talking about is how successful their coping devices are, not whether they

48

really enjoy what they do. Nor are most workers — aware of few other employment opportunities, and having already invested fifteen or twenty years in the same occupation — willing to say that their entire life's work has been a waste of time.

Isolated in specific occupational tasks, how are workers to confront management over quality of work conditions? Trained in high schools and universities which view occupations as apolitical entities, how are most workers to gain a knowledge that things can be better, that there are alternatives?

Yet, perhaps the major deterrent to escaping an occupational coping pattern is that quality of work problems, like problems of unemployment, are conceptualized by most workers as personal in character. We, rather than the corporation who employs us, are to blame for any lack of meaning or failure of adjustment to corporate goals. In much the same way, high school and college students come to blame themselves for failure to find excitement and interest in their classes. If we are held responsible for our situation, but at the same time can do nothing about that situation, cannot decide what we will produce, what job we will take, then we remain powerless, yet do not recognize the basis of our impotence. As a result, there is nothing we can do but cope.

On the other hand, if we refuse to acknowledge our problem as only personal in nature, but rather define the structure and leadership of the corporate organizations which employ us as the problem, then we open up the possibility of addressing the root causes of our dilemma, the reasons why our job is not meaningful, the reasons why we are powerless. If the corporation is responsible for the lack of high quality employment, then the issue is more than a personal problem since the corporation affects more than one individual.

Confronting the problem of alienating work then would mean banding together with other alienated workers to gain power over basic corporate decisions: what is to be produced, how is it to be produced, who is going to do the producing, and how much profit everyone will make.

Yet few workers are ready to take this step, or even recognize it as a viable option. So much easier to cope with the situation, rather than try and change it, so much easier and safer, for if we confront the corporate leaders, we also run the risk of losing our jobs. So much easier in terms of the values we have all been raised on, to "do our own thing", be an individualist on the inside, inside our head, than risk losing that sense of individuality by joining together with others to gain power within the bureau-cracy. So much easier and safer to let ourselves be co-opted, to think of ourselves as independent and self-sufficient, than to risk losing that sense of individual prowess by identifying the corporation as the problem which must be changed for real independence and self-worth to take root and grow. So much easier to let the corporation do what it wants, to passively accept its priorities, and to buy a meaningful identity elsewhere . . .

Department-Stor-Ism: Buying a Trouble Free Identity

4

Our job may not mean very much, but it's nice to have that paycheck at the end of the week, nice to be able to pay our house mortgage, make our car payment, have the refrigerator stocked, and nice to be able to buy other things — a new car, dress, sports coat, tea set, record album, t.v., shoes, pantyhose, perfume, tie, chain saw, watch — as well. Most employment may not leave us with a sense of accomplishment, a feeling of pride and self-worth, but the money we receive for our efforts enables us to purchase these feelings elsewhere, or, at least, to think that we can. Consumerism has become a primary way of coping for those of us unable to find meaning in our occupational task. The need to purchase products goes far beyond the desire to feel good about ourselves, or to find values lost in the workplace — individualism, competition, independence — rather, consumerism is a necessity, a part of doing our duty, being a good citizen in American society, for without the constant purchasing of new products, the economy would collapse. It is, after all, no secret that corporations are able to stay in business only if they make a profit. In order to gain such monetary rewards, they need to sell products — either new products to old customers, or tried and tested items to new customers. Without these sales, profits go down, and workers are laid off. We lose our jobs. There is little need to worry, for in a rather clever fashion, corporations insure that their goods will be purchased (often by their very employees), by making work boring, repetitive and without meaning. Unable to find a worthwhile identity on the job, we are forced to cope with this sense of loss by buying an identity elsewhere. Alienating work thus guarantees corporate profits and, coming full circle, a steady job manufacturing the items of our own salvation.

Most corporations which sell consumer products don't gamble on our ability to reason out the correlation between buying and employment. Rather, they capitalize on the type of identity most of us have been led to expect from our jobs, and through various forms of advertising show how such an identity can be gained from a visit to a nearby shopping center. The worker who thought his job might give him a sense of independence is thus urged to smoke Marlboros, wear faded jeans (during off hours), and drive a new Mustang. Independence in corporate advertising is also equated with rebellion, the need to be different, to achieve a distinct status. Though millions of persons may be buying the same product, each customer is made to feel as though the item he or she is paying for has been designed especially for them, for their own *individual* needs. Independence is also equated with being in control, since control and power are what is so often lacking in corporate and factory employment. An ad depicting a man peeling out of the driveway or speeding down the freeway in his new Dodge shows us how to gain control, how to take charge.

Our control is also manifested by the way in which we manipulate the market — getting a good deal on what we purchase. When we come home from a busy day at the shopping center and tell our wife, husband or neighbor that we hit a terrific sale, we are doing more than telling them that we have saved money. Rather, we are showing them how we beat the system, how wise and cunning we have been. Nobody is going to take advantage of us. Besides, we point out, the price may go up any day, so it was better to buy now even if we have to live beyond our means for a little while. You have to spend money to make money. It is in such shopping practice, and the calculation of how much we are going to save, that the Protestant Work Ethic we found so difficult to gain meaning from at our place of employment becomes adapted to the time and energy we spend as consumers. No need to feel guilty for not doing our fair share at the office, for we make our contribution on Saturday afternoons at the Mall.

Being independent and being in control is also assumed to be a part of the male identity. Though one cannot dominate his workplace, or tell others what to do, with the help of a new *masculine* deodorant, one can easily push his woman around, make her respect you, let her know who's boss. Indeed, a great many television and billboard advertisements deliver this very message: boost your male ego by drinking Seagram's, then dominate the woman of your choice. For family men, a sign of self-support and strength is someone who doesn't let their home run down, who builds a $10,000 machine shop in his garage and uses it twice a year to build bookshelves for the kids or an extension on the deck. He is also someone who takes care of his family: Don't let *your* wife use the wrong detergent when she washes *your* clothes, a masculine voice tells the busy housewife or drive in the rain with the wrong tires on her car; and what if someday you're gone, dead, in the ground forever and there's no one to make these payments — don't let your family down, buy life insurance today. A good family man is also someone who is constantly looking around for a bigger and better house to move his family into, in a neighborhood where you're treated with respect, where you know *who you are.*

The housewife, tired of assembly-line dishes, laundry, kids' problems, floor problems, dusting, and chauffeuring, is also offered relief. How much easier those household tasks become if you had a new set of kitchen cabinets, if you could vacuum your living room rug with a new Kirby, if you had a Maytag, or could cover up those leftovers with Handiwrap. Coping with household drudgery, of course, means more than buying new products to do the same old tasks; it also means feeling good about oneself as a woman. How much better it feels to take oneself down to the department store and find a new dress, one that will make your husband sit up and take notice, or a new bath oil so that your skin will feel silky soft again. And if your husband doesn't pay attention, maybe someone else will.

Coping through buying is effective because it supplies instant gratification. No need to take long years rebuilding one's personality, taking dancing lessons, trying to find a better job. No need to pay now, either. Credit cards have enabled the average American to get whatever he needs today, never mind that we might not have the financial resources to foot the bill, interest payments will more than make up for the inconvenience till we do. Yet the identity we buy today may be worthless tomorrow — the new suit we felt so good about yesterday, now lying lifeless in the closet, buried alongside the shirt we so desperately had to have. It's not that the suit doesn't fit, or the shirt doesn't match our new shoes, it's just that we're tired of it; it just doesn't seem to mean as much, it's just that we need a *new* one. The identities we purchase so easily with our credit cards are just as easily lost, for the material appendages we would use to bolster our shattered egos can never be more than the lifeless ingredients from which they are made. Superfluous consumer goods, since they do not deal directly with our on-the-job problems, can never give us the satisfaction of having done so, despite what the advertisements for these goods have promised. The difficulty, however, is that the man who fails to find his individuality in the purchase of a new car, his independence in a new aftershave lotion, or power from his skilsaw, does not ask himself whether there is something the matter with the method he has used to gain the feelings of individuality, independence and power — that is, with the process of superfluous consumption he has practiced — rather, he blames the product for its failure to deliver, and goes out and buys a new brand. As alienating work leads to dependence on superfluous consumption as a way of coping so too, alienating purchases — items we no longer like or feel good about — necessitate continued buying as we search for a product that does feel right. Since by definition there is no such product, the continued purchase of alienating commodities must go on indefinitely.

Yet, how can we be mistaken, when everyone else is doing it, when the shopping centers are jammed on Saturday afternoons, when department stores keep sending us new credit cards in the mail? And, if we are wrong, then how are we to justify our investments, the items we have already stockpiled in our garage and closet, the bills we still owe out? How could we have been so foolish? Better not to admit it, better to pretend that nothing is the matter, to carry on.

III

One of the major appeals of corporate advertisements is that the purchase of a given commodity will enhance our relationships. "If he kissed you once, will he kiss you again? Be certain, try Certs." In fact, much of the reason for enhancing our identities as independent, take-control men, and demure, insecure, deodorized women is to match public and corporate images of the kind of people who make good bed partners and potential mates. Why do we need such consumer goods to show off our personalities, to enhance our status and attractiveness in the eyes of a potential loved one? Part of the reason is because we already use consumer goods to bolster our work-impaired identity, so it is easy to adapt it as a lifestyle when attempting to relate to members of the opposite sex. Perhaps, more significant, however, is that our interpersonal relationships have become more important than ever because, for many of us, they are the only thing left that defines us as having a meaningful identity and being a meaningful person. This is not only because corporate and factory employment does not match our expectations, but there are few other aspects of American society where we can find equal sustenance. We have never been a particularly political populace, as readily demonstrated by our educational system, nor do most people find a sense of fulfillment from organized religion. As a result, we now increasingly rely on our relationships to make up for occupational and spiritual losses, for the lack of purpose many of us sense in our lives. Unfortunately, this places a tremendous amount of pressure on these relationships to succeed and to fulfill all of our needs. The nuclear family — husband, wife, two kids. — was never designed to achieve such a goal. But no matter, because there is nowhere else for us to turn anyway, no other place to take our grievances, so it must succeed; we must find an ideal relationship. To make sure that we do not fail, to stand beside us in our moment of need, corporations provide an array of products which guarantee satisfaction, or you can buy a more expensive brand. And with so much at stake, why take a chance, why not use everything at your disposal?

It is possible that the purchase of a new dress, a different kind of mascara, or a new sport coat will attract someone of the opposite sex, because this is what everyone expects that they will do, and such products do make us more physically attractive. Then, as the saying goes, once attracted, we will have a chance to let our real selves hang out, to show off our personality, our "inner beauty". In some cases this is no doubt true, for if wearing a new dress makes us feel better about ourselves, then this positive self-image will be reflected in our conversation, and our general enthusiasm for life. As a result, we will make a better impression and it will probably give us greater courage to approach those whom we might have formerly felt were "out of reach". For many of us, reliance on consumer goods to establish a relationship leads to continued reliance on ever newer products so we never look "bad" in the eyes of the one we love. Can we get ourselves all duded up to go to a bar or party, hustle someone who likes the way we look and what we drive, and then pretend that none of this will make any difference in the long run, when we both wake up in the morning without our wardrobes on?

But there is more to a consumer orientation than the way we dress and what we drive. Many relationships are established and maintained not because of the way someone looks in our eyes, but the way they look in public, at the "right" bars, restaurants, and discos. The couple that must dine out or go drinking every night, so they won't sit home and deal with each other, so they won't have to ever "undress", uses food and drink as a way of coping with what would otherwise be a dismal relationship. They must, of course, continue to purchase the latest fashions, so as not to appear out of place. Yet, a consumer orientation is not only necessary for many young marrieds, or swinging singles, but many a housewife finds it necessary to constantly dress up as well, lest she lose her husband to a secretary at work, or someone he might meet at a bar after the office has closed.

Relationships add to the consumer impulse in other ways as well. If we are dependent on one other person, our husband or wife or lover, to give our lives a sense of meaning or purpose, to satisfy all our needs, then it seems only natural that many relationships will fail. The rising divorce statistics indicate, in fact, that this is the case. Unfortunately, the increase in broken marriages has not caused us to re-examine whether or not any one person can ever truly satisfy all of our needs, whether they can take the place of empty jobs or purposeless educations. On the contrary, while the divorce rate is on the increase, so too are the number of marriages and living together arrangements. With relationships in constant flux all around us, it makes it difficult for many couples to ever settle down to acknowledge to each other that they are no longer out looking for somebody else. Consequently, the security once found in marital vows has been replaced by the nagging insecurity that it can happen anytime. One day he'll come home from the office and pack his bags, or we'll go to a dinner party and she'll up and leave with my best friend. Marital insecurity leads to constant consumerism as both husband and wife feel the need to make themselves attractive; more attractive than potential competition. It also means that they must always look available, just in case. The more pressure each member of a relationship feels to prove that they are the best of all possible mates, the more jealous each becomes of the other's activities, and of the potential threat posed by strangers and even friends. This leads to a vicious cycle in which the question of our husband or wife's fidelity — especially in the face of already having made ourselves as attractive as possible — now necessitates that we work even harder, purchasing a newer perfume, a more expensive dress, a more masculine cologne, blow dryer, or dinner for two — in order to hold onto the relationship. Initial insecurity leads to constant distrust and the constant need to prove our love. How better to show her that you care than by buying her a . . . . by Revlon. Like the man who purchases a new car to prove he still has it, the quick way to marital or relationship security becomes an ever newer look, to maintain the old excitement.

Buying has also become a way of patching up relationships, of quickly settling family quarrels. No need to waste hours of time hassling, just stop in and get her a new dress on your way home from work. Have a great steak and his favorite bottle of wine waiting on the table when he comes through the door, even though you may have just put in a forty-hour week yourself. In spite of the fact that most women now work, the same relationship roles are often maintained—the woman in the kitchen, the man in front of the t.v. set drinking a beer, or reading the paper. Yet, the return of women to work or school has added to relationship insecurity. This is especially a problem for husbands, who, unable to keep their wives safe at home, must now adjust to the possibility that they might meet other men, might form their own friendships, might find someone more interesting, attractive, or stimulating to be with.

Not only do we try and patch up marital quarrels through quick purchases, but we often attempt to make up for inept child-rearing by attempting to buy our children's love. If we've been working all week and haven't had a chance to play with our kids, or have spent our free hours with our husband or wife, then what easier way to make it up to them than by taking them to the toystore, or, if that will take too much time, then just picking something up for them to surprise them with at breakfast. This is a similar syndrome to that which divorced fathers often go through, having lost custody of their children to their former wives. Only able to see their children once a month, or every other weekend, they attempt to make up for lost time by spending as much money as possible on whatever their children desire. The more gifts purchased, the greater your child will love you, or so the reasoning goes, and the less he or she will love their mother. This of course greatly complicates things for mom, when the kids come home and demand the same sort of favors and goodies as dad has just supplied.

Consumer goods also help make up for friendships we have not maintained and relatives we rarely see. This is especially the case around Christmas time, when we rush through department stores looking for something they will like, anything, providing we can charge it. For our little girl cousins there are thousands of dolls and miniature make-up kits to show them the kind of people they should be like when they grow up; the kind of beauty they should emulate. For the boys, there are space cities to take their minds off their school problems, to occupy themselves with when we are not there to visit with them. The more lavish the gift, the more they will remember us--that's the uncle who gave me a Barbie Town House and the Holly Hobbie Craft Center. For our friends too we need something unique, something that's just right for them, a special perfume, dress, candle, pipe or decanter. We were going to write them all letters this year, put little notes in their stockings promising to help them mow the lawn, paint their house, take them to the park, give them a massage, but there just wasn't the time, and they wouldn't have appreciated it anyway. It's just not the same as unwrapping a big box. And as Christmas Day gets closer, we push and shove others in line at the cash register, grabbing whatever is closest to us, worrying about who we will give it to later. At least we haven't forgotten anyone.

The need to set ourselves up with just one other person in nuclear family units, and the increase in divorce and single parent families means that we must each have one of everything. Each family must have its own t.v., washing machine, lawn mower, car, dishes, and vacuum cleaner. In the same way, as we noted earlier, the emphasis on individualism and independence at the shopping center means that each of us must have our own individually tailored wardrobe. Under the Christmas tree, each of us must have our own gifts. Families do not share, just as individuals do not share, unless of course they are a couple living together.

To share is to compromise oneself, to give up part of one's identity; it is to lose one's independence. A family cannot share what they have with other families because that would show that the husband is unable to take care of his wife and kids, that he is not a man, that he is not strong. A woman is often unwilling to share, because every other woman is a potential threat to her marital security, in competition for her husband or boyfriend. Equally important, if everyone else has what we have, then how can we say we are distinct, unique . . . our own person? If everyone else can share what we have, then *who* can we say we are?

At the same time, nuclear family units, single parent families, or a singles lifestyle, keep us alone and isolated, powerless to change, unable to get support for other options, and for confronting problems which cause us to adapt consumerism as a coping mechanism in the first place. Our *individual* purchases also enable corporations to make profits, and for all of us to keep our jobs.

IV

Like the worker who copes with an alienating occupation by identifying with the larger corporation which employs him, and the student who rationalizes a boring and irrelevant education by saying "I'm at Michigan," we often attempt to justify our excessive consumer behavior by equating our individual purchase with the American ideal of progress. The kind of progress we are talking about, however, is not toward some greater humanitarian goal, such as world peace. On the contrary, we are speaking about technological progress. The products we help manufacture may not in themselves mean a great deal, but who hasn't walked down a brightly lit department store aisle crammed full with ever more sophisticated gadgets, new types of synthetic fabrics, foods that need no preparation, that cook themselves while we are riding down the freeway, microwave ovens, vacuum cleaners that do the dishes while they are cleaning off the counter top; who has not seen such a technological array and not felt his heart gladden at the sight, proud of America, proud of our technological ingenuity? Indeed, as many historians have noted, America has always been inordinately successful in creating a machine which will solve all problems, whether the problem is technological in character, or sociological. The solution to buzzing flies is a bug bomb, the solution for being unable to find a good relationship is to substitute our car as the object of our affection, and the solution to international conflict is the development of nuclear bombs, it makes no difference. The difficulty is that technological solutions to non-technological problems are not particularly effective, since they do not address the causes of the problem. Nuclear bombs have not brought lasting peace, only the threat of massive annihilation. Consumer gadgets may mean technological progress, but they haven't solved the problems enumerated in this chapter, the problem of finding a meaningful identity in a purposeful and worthwhile community and society.

And yet, technological progress does save us time. It *is* less work to wash clothing in a washing machine than by hand; to have wrinkle free shirts than to have to iron them; to be able to cook a meal in a microwave oven, than wait the additional time it might take to prepare it in a traditional stove. In the same way, it saves time if we can repair a relationship by buying something for the one whom we have offended. And time is an important commodity, for with so much of it wasted at work, we have so little left over to make use of, with which to prove ourselves.

If newer and fancier gadgets are being produced, if American society is moving forward, then so too are we. Science may yet save us, may yet find a solution to the boring job, in automation for example, so why should we lose faith now? Yet, automation has also led to unemployment . . . .

Technology in some ways has become the great equalizer, granting everyone the same opportunity to achieve the identity of their choice. Freedom and equality for all, one of the cornerstone tenets of American society, becomes fulfilled at the local Macys. How easy to be whoever you want just at the snap of a credit card. Join the Dodge rebellion, drive a new Charger; be an Islander, buy puca shells; be for peace with your new peace medallion; be liberated with your new natural look make-up—but underneath it all, be no one. For those who would use the handcrafted items of their own labor to present a public image, mass production stereotypes of their efforts serve to destroy the identity they would achieve, and the individual they would seek to preserve. The use of politically and culturally defiant rhetoric to sell consumer goods, co-opts potential dissent and eliminates the impact it might have, as the words peace and revolution come to be used in a myriad of ways and to sell a variety of products. As a result, it becomes difficult to establish a distinct power base, a rallying point for those who truly believe, for those who stand for something, who wear faded jeans because they do not want to spend their money on a new pair, and because they want to let others know that appearance is not important. Since we can no longer distinquish people we come in contact with by style dress or rhetoric, it becomes difficult to trust anyone else, to know who we are dealing with—hippie? liberator? cop? housewife? salesman? And yet, the more we look alike, the more we are perhaps forced to present ourselves in other ways, in fashions which go beyond our outside appearance.

Technology has also enabled more well-to-do senior members to our society to cope with the problem of aging by trying to look young again, for the younger we are, the further away from death we become. Youth also represents a period in our lives when we supposedly had everything going for us, when we could do whatever we wanted, when we were as beautiful and handsome as the television ads. But there are only a few wealthy seniors. For the rest, having followed a lifetime of consumer coping, of feeling guilty for not having purchased enough, a fixed income retirement and meager social security pension make it impossible to continue the lifestyle that has been giving their lives meaning. How else might they demonstrate their allegiance to American society? How else can they atone for the increased emptiness they now feel as members of the permanently unemployed?

There is more to a consumer lifestyle than the constant purchase of new products, and the values which are attached to this process. There is a leisure consumption as well, the buying of new experiences, new record albums, new concerts, new dope, new therapy, new kinds of meals to cook, new bars to drink in, new ski slopes to run, and new people to make love to. There is nothing wrong with any of these activities in themselves. Yet, as we will see in subsequent chapters, they detract our energies and attention away from our problems and do not offer a solution in return. They make it easy to fade out, to be absorbed in the beat of the music on the stereo, the exhiliration of the feel of the snow speeding beneath us, the pounding sound of a rock concert, and the drinks mellow inside of us. These activities often entertain us, but many times we give nothing in return; we listen to *their* music, and then we put another album on. Our reliance on such experiential consumption also means that we must be on the constant lookout for new ways to get turned-on, so we can avoid creating our own sources of excitement and gratification. And the more they involve us, the less capacity we have to go elsewhere, to escape the web of pleasure which surrounds us, enveloping us in a fog, manipulating our senses. Soon our problems no longer matter, as a cash register in someone else's hands rings up another sale; a $7.95 concert ticket, a new ski parka, three more drinks. Technology too will bring us new highs, new amusement park rides, new auras to lose ourselves in. But once lost, who will bring us back? And who will control the society while we are gone?

* * *

Reliance on superfluous consumption, whether of a material or experiential kind, is a coping mechanism because it does not enable us to solve our problems. And once hooked, once our energies are directed toward the nearest shopping center or rock concert, then how much do we have left over to consider alternative ways of dealing with these problems? How open do we remain for other solutins? Yet the more we buy, the less comfortable we feel, for there is always something we must yet purchase.

Turning Ourselves Off: Television, The Easy Escape

5

Imagine coming home from a hard day at the office. You're living alone and a moment or two after you walk into your apartment you flip on the t.v. A face immediately appears on the screen, a casually dressed gentleman, sitting in an overstuffed chair in a living room, sipping a martini. It's cocktail hour, and as you pour yourself a glass of wine, and sit on the couch in *your* living room, the face on the screen asks: "Have a difficult day?" As you make a move to nod, the voice continues, "I did. First the computer broke down, and . . . ." The man on the screen keeps talking, describing a busy rush hour commute, interspersed with general questions about what might have happened to you. After a half hour or so, and several commercial interruptions, he is joined by a couple of kids and a nicely dressed woman who tells him that dinner is ready. The t.v. dinner you have placed in the oven during one of the commercials is also now ready and as they sit down at their table, you join them at yours. Conversation begins, and you are included. Major news events are brought up, the kids talk about what went on in school, the woman comments on who called, or about what happened to her at work. Upcoming television shows are discussed, and as dinner concludes, the family on the screen adjourns to their family room to watch their favorite shows, inviting you to join them.

I

Sound fanciful? The average household in America has their television set on six hours a day. In fact, in many homes, the television stays on even though no one may be watching. For the housewife stuck home alone, the sound of the set and an occasional fleeting glance at the screen is probably reassuring; "someone" else is there with her to share the drudgery, to make her feel more secure. Many singles also have the t.v. on from the moment they come home so they too will not feel isolated, cut off from the rest of the world, nor is it uncommon for some to leave the set on all night, though they are not awake to watch the late night movie and the early morning farm report.

Yet, to the vast majority of Americans, television represents an escape, a way of coping with an unpleasant job, boring classes, and trying relationships. By immersing ourselves in the t.v. screen, becoming mesmerized by the action taking place before us, we no longer have to worry about who we are, and what we are doing with our own lives. Nor do we have to give anything up, to lose control, to risk our individuality. For no one is telling us what to do, they are only showing us what they are doing, and if we don't like it, we can always change the channel. It is a way of having our cake and eating it too, for we can have our individuality, without having to prove ourselves; communication without compromise; communion without sharing. It is the best of all possible worlds.

Television also uses up time so we don't have to work on solving problems. In a similar sense it provides a ready baby sitting service to keep our children happy, pacified and out of the way so their gentle voices will not disturb whatever activities we have planned or must get done. This has become especially important because many parents, already frustrated by alienating jobs, have little left over to give their kids at the end of the day. Far easier just to turn on the tube, and not have to worry about it. Nor are housewives, having spent most of the day saddled with chores, always in the mood to entertain their school aged children, who, having been forced to be passive class-room receptors all day, burst through the front door ready for some action.

As such, television viewing has become a vehicle around which to organize our lives, something we can look forward to, and count on, when the chips are down. It is not uncommon for school kids to get their homework done early so they can watch their favorite reruns at five o'clock, or for a family to become accustomed to watching the news together during dinner, or to plan their social schedule around their most popular shows so they won't miss anything, especially when one week's viewing is determined by what happened the previous week, as is the case with many of the soap opera serials. (Video replay machines, however, may solve this problem.) While the defenders of family viewing claim that television gives the family something in common, something they can all do together, others point out that what they are doing together is avoiding each other. Weekends too, cease to be a problem, a stretch of time to be filled, especially for men, who readily turn family rooms on Saturday and Sunday afternoons into football, basketball, or baseball stadiums, seizing control of the set just as their offspring have finished a four-hour cartoon marathon.

II

There are many reasons why television viewing enables us to escape. One of the most pervasive is that many shows provide a sense of adventure for the vast majority of us who lead adventureless lives. Watching a detective stalk a killer, our blood pressure pounding in our temples, hands gripping the edge of the couch (or a bottle of diet Pepsi) is certainly far more thrilling than processing forms at the insurance company which employs us. It is also a great deal more enthralling than diagramming a sentence in our junior high school class, or reading about Mesopotamia. Yet, the adventure we would vicariously identify with by fixing our eyes on the color screen involves little risk. The characters in the crime drama may be involved in a life and death struggle, but we are not. As a result, though the criminal is finally apprehended or shot in the end, we may feel little sense of closure, that *something* has actually happened, that *our* lives have been transformed. But we need not worry, because after a brief commercial interruption, we can immerse ourselves in a new plot, a new crime, disease, or family problem. It is only at the end of the evening, when we tiredly crawl between the sheets, that we may feel let down, that there is something different between the actions which highlight our lives and the adventures which face our t.v. companions. And it is only then that we may feel frustrated, because the coping mechanism we have engaged in has not readily dealt with the lack of stimulation in our own situation.

Yet, many of us do not want to lead adventuresome lives; do not want to run risks, because we are having enough trouble handling the insecurities we already face. For us, t.v. adventure must serve the function of entertainment, and entertainment which requires no effort. All we need do is sit on our couches, and the medium will absorb us, pulling us out of our doldrums, making us laugh or cry, or simply enabling us to relax, indifferent to what's on, expecting nothing in return for the service it has rendered. Plots are often designed accordingly, focusing around specific, easily identifiable situations which require little effort to figure out. The motivations of characters are readily understood, and the drama revolves around a cause and effect scheme which allows solutions of the "situation" in a twenty minute period of time. Loose ends are tied up, and we can go to bed without having to worry about what actually happened. Closure, in this case, is important, since without such a sense of completion, we might again feel out of control, that events are taking place about which we have little understanding, leaving in question an outcome that we are powerless to determine.

III

Besides the fact that we spend an inordinate amount of time watching television — whether it be for a lost sense of adventure or for pure entertainment — as a means of escaping from having to deal with our problems, the content of television viewing material also affects the way in which we confront pressing issues in our "real" lives. A large number of prime time television shows, for example, revolve around cops and robbers plots of one type or another. These entail everything from police morticians to detectives to patrolmen, from cops who break the law to get their "man", to those who don't, and from private detectives to counter-espionage agents. What do these shows tell us in terms of how to solve problems?

The first "insight" we get is that we shouldn't deal with crime problems at all, rather, we should let the police handle them. This is all well and good for most of us, because we would just as soon have professionals deal with those issues so that we can get on with the real business at hand — finding personal satisfaction.

Directly related to having professionals solve crime problems for us is the idea that we are being protected at all times by an able-bodied police force. While crime may be on the increase, for every criminal there's a crafty detective or plain clothes man to catch them, therefore, there's nothing we need worry about, no need to feel insecure, to put an extra latch on the front door. But even more important for how such programs enable us to cope with a problematic social environment is the manner in which crime itself is portrayed.

Most television crimes are street crimes, that is, they involve burglary or homicide. No effort is made to justify crime on the basis of societal causes — someone knocking over a gas station in order to get enough money to buy food for his starving family, or in order to make the house payment — actions which, from another perspective, are coping mechanisms of the poor. Rather, crimes are committed by dishonest or immoral individuals who deserve to get caught. Moreover, most crimes do not have complex motives; on the contrary, as we noted earlier, they are single-minded acts taking place in a twenty minute format, which are *always* solved. Nor are white collar or political crime extensively portrayed.

How many shows have we seen that deal with corporate price fixing, or collusion between political and business interests? Social problems which may affect our lives, then, are depicted as personal acts of a dishonest or immoral character, having no societal derivation, and which are easily solved by professionals. The message seems clear: we are responsible for our own actions and if we get out of hand, the police will arrest us. The way to be a good person in American society is to lead a clean and upright existence; the way to cope with social pressure is not to break the law. Yet, we want *someone* to break the law, for how else might we be entertained, engrossed by the chase, fascinated by the deviance?

Medical shows deliver much the same message: doctors can cure most any problem. Since all health problems have a medical derivation, that is, they are physiologically caused, the medical profession warrants our trust and confidence. Unfortunately, as in most cases of criminality, many illnesses are generated by societal conditions requiring social action. Doctors may be able to treat the symptoms — restore a heart patient to normal breathing, temporarily arrest the cancer — but they cannot prevent thousands of other persons from coming down with these same maladies, for they do not address the high pressure work pace, the social insecurities, and toxic factory conditions which cause these diseases to occur in the first place. Yet medical shows, reflecting real life medical interest, never concern themselves with causes, because that would mean that doctors could no longer be relied on to have THE cure. As a result, people would panic over what to do about an illness they were experiencing: whom could they turn to? It would also mean that individuals would have to begin confronting the social conditions that gave rise to their physiological symptoms. What is there about my job that makes me feel anxious all the time? Why can't I sleep at night? For a media based on enabling people to cope, such questions

76

would be irresponsible at best, and seditious at worst. Better off letting us believe that doctors can cure everyone and be able to relax.

Medical and crime shows also serve to remind us how efficient technology is in dealing with our problems. Elaborate operations are staged nightly before our very eyes, or detectives go over fingerprint tests from the lab in their effort to apprehend the latest villain. The drivers of police cars are always better trained, their cars always faster, their minds brighter than those of their adversaries. How reassuring, if only it were true. Despite technological advances, most t.v. crimes are solved through violence — someone gets killed, not caught. While technological and rational solutions are nice, they are often too abstract. How much easier just to get down to it, get it over with right away, solve the problem once and for all. How the viewer often longs for such solutions, not to have to worry what the reason for it was, just to do it. Cut and dried. How good it feels to get out the anger, to bare one's frustrations, to kill the enemy — even if it isn't the assembly line, the boss, one's wife or child. How much more stimulating. Yet, at the end of such a solution, having watched the protagonists fight it out, no holds barred, where is *our* release since it is not *our* violence? Having risked nothing, we get nothing in return.

Violence also permeates the cartoon shows our offspring view every Saturday morning. In fact, it is unusual to see such animated displays without watching a raccoon, cat, pig, or mouse being annihilated several dozen times in the course of a five minute episode. Yet here, violence does not end the conflict; rather, no matter how many times an animal is blown to bits, they always seem to bounce back, the show ending with one of the protagonists too exhausted to go on, not because they are no longer physically capable of renting any more damage.

Yet, while violence dominates television crime shows and cartoons alike, it can only leave us frustrated. One of the messages conveyed through such programming is that physical brutality is a way of solving our personal problems. Someone gets in your way, all you have to do is "off them." The difficulty is that we are not supposed to be violent; rather, we are supposed to work out our problems through discussion and conciliation. Watching actors on television shoot it out, then, can only leave us hanging, viewing such action as a possible solution, but unable to put it into practice in "real life".

Another drawback to the use of violence as a solution to some of our frustrations is that it isn't really a solution to these problems at all — even if we are motivated to adopt it as a strategy. For one thing, how can we solve problems of alienating work, marital conflict, irrelevant school curriculums and unemployment by beating someone up or shooting a manager? What might typically happen is that the manager we disfigure will only be replaced by another manager having the same philosophy as the one we would intimidate. Moreover, we would probably be arrested. Even more important, violence fails as a way of confronting our problems because it is a *personal* solution to what is often a societal or social issue. Attempting to fight a bureaucracy by injuring one of its members leaves us as powerless as doing nothing at all. We might have temporarily vented our anger, but the problem remains. So we keep watching our televisions, excited by the battling actors we see before us, yet unable to adapt what we see on our screens as solutions to our problems.

IV

Most of us are neither faced with a major illness nor perpetrators or victims of a crime. Rather, we are concerned with the day-to-day exigencies of our lives and how we can cope with the *personal* problems we run up against. A variety of television programs are ostensibly geared toward people just like us. These situation comedies and soap operas attempt to make our everyday world interesting by getting us to laugh at how serious we may take even the small things, or by showing us that other people are faced with the same personal issues as we are.

Thus, we watch a middle class family deal with the family dog who goes to the bathroom on the floor, or a girl on her first date, or an affair someone is having. What is characteristic about these shows is, again, that the problems are always of a personal nature — society is never the culprit. At best, as in the case of a few family shows, there is a communication problem between family members — never are family problems seen as a microcosm or symptom of occupational and educational pressures or boredom.

Moreover, problems always reach a satisfactory solution: all affairs must come to an end if one is already married; the dog must stop going to the bathroom; the child must do her homework. Such shows enable us to cope by telling us that we are not alone in the problems we face, or in the situations in which we find ourselves; we too can solve our pressing problems. Yet, are all of us financially well off, do all of our problems revolve around who is going to take the family car for the evening? What about other problems we may be faced with, but which are ignored by the screen in front of us? Unemployment. Occupational alienation. School boredom. Consumerism. Can these issues be so easily dealt with? Can *personal* action alone solve these problems? Yet, to adequately deal with these issues might make us feel uncomfortable, make us want to change channels, or turn the set off altogether. Their solution might also require that we organize collectively with others to gain greater power. Where has such collective involvement been portrayed on the 21-inch tube? Where in the *TV Guide* are shows called *Community Organizer, Social Reformer, Sociological Therapist?*

There are also numerous shows which attempt to take us back to a simpler era, where men were men and women knew their place; a time when problems could be easily ironed out, when families didn't have to concern themselves with extramarital relationships and divorce, when children went to school like they were supposed to, and everyone could be seen in church on Sunday morning. The Waltons and many of the Disney programs are prime examples of this kind of television fare. Remember the good ol' days, when life had purpose and meaning? Yet, when the set goes off, and we look around our family rooms, or our apartments, where is the old farm house that the Waltons live in, the snow covered fields, the large family seated around a table?

How does watching the "simpler" problems experienced in their lives enable us to deal with problems we face in ours? Can we turn the clock back? Obviously not, but we often wish that we could. What such programs also fail to relate is that events were not as idealistically solved forty years ago as the Waltons would have us believe. Personal and social problems were equally complicated both in analysis and in solution. It is only in retrospect that those years become simpler in character, entertaining, though of little help in wrestling with our own dilemmas.

V

Television programming enables us to escape and be entertained in other ways as well. Perhaps the most intriguing manner in which this is done is through the evening news. News shows, as most of us are aware, are divided into local news and national/international news stories. They are typically aired during dinner — 5:30 - 7:30 — and after prime time broadcasting has ended — 11:00 - 11:30. What is especially important about dinner time newscasting is that it be of such a nature so as not to give anyone indigestion, yet interesting enough to hold the viewer's attention. Local news focuses on fires, crimes, and statements by politicans, with a few minutes left over for a special interest feature, for example, how a new corporation changed a small town. While newscasters maintain that the purpose of the news is to inform, little mention is ever made as to what individuals are to do with the information that is conveyed, nor is the viewer directly involved in the events he sees before him on the screen. As a result, the television audience can tell itself it is keeping up with what's happening in the world, yet they do not have to do anything about any of the problems they see portrayed; nor are they expected to. A family can eat their evening meal, content in the fact that they do not have to converse with each other, and at the same time feel good about being "informed citizens", by acquainting themselves with the day's important events.

Yet, most news shows are not very informative. The knowledgeable citizens we would become will not be based on the information gleaned from an evening newscast. Like television crime shows, the evening news focuses on spectacular and typically violent events. A highjacking in Turkey, a flood in Iowa, the murder of three women in Detroit, a local fire or burglary; perhaps a statement by the President on the Middle East crisis. What do these events have to do with our lives? Where is the news about the personal problems we face and what people are doing about them? Where on the evening news are social problems being analyzed in depth, and actions depicted which show how these problems are being solved? It is one thing to talk about a murder or a fire, and quite another to discuss what is being done so that these fires and crimes do not occur again.

How many newscasters take the time to explain how inflation will affect the average person; how unemployment is a social problem which affects us all; how occupational alienation affects problems we might be having in our family? News events are depicted as being isolated incidents. Crimes which happen one week have no relation to those which happen the following week, no underlying causes link the two situations. Nor is there any attempt to make a connection between different events occurring the same evening, for example, a rise in unemployment and an increase in the price of food. And sandwiched in between these different bits of information are several minutes of commercials, none of which typically relate to the content of the news, though a clever anchorman might certainly draw some comparison.

The end result of this kind of newsscasting is to leave the viewer outside the situations portrayed in front of him. It is not his fire, he is not the victim of a crime, he is not unemployed, and if he is, the news he has probably witnessed does not relate to the problems he currently faces. Isolated from fragmented news events, the viewer has considerable difficulty relating the news to problems he experiences in his own life. Consequently, he emerges from watching such a program with no greater awareness of the community, city, and world situation, than he had before turning on the set. He is also powerless, because the news has not told him how to solve problems he sees on the screen, nor has it provided him with an in-depth analysis on which to base political and social action. Like his situation at work, or his kids' situation at school, he has no chance of talking back to his television news show, no way he can ask questions, or debate the purpose of what he has just seen. The news, then, comes to blend in with the rest of the evening's viewing, the real merges with the unreal, an actual crime with one that has been fictionally portrayed. In between are commercials which are in neither world. Does diet Pepsi really attract boys? Will Brut actually make the ladies fall all over you? Ironically, it may be these very commercials which are the only part of an evening's program which directly relate to our own lives, which directly tell us what to do to solve OUR problems.

It is here that the chief message of television comes across. Television prepares us to be consumers, passive receivers of commercial announcements, news events, life's adventures and conflicts. The way to cope is to turn oneself off, and turn the television on. And like consumerism, we can always buy another brand, we can always change channels, but we can never stop watching, turn in our credit cards, unplug the set. While there are clear exceptions to the overall nature of television programming — the CBS special on the coal industry, or nuclear energy; the Xerox-sponsored Ibsen play — these events are so far apart, and are such rare occurrences, that they become almost like the high school social problems class a few of us took one year, and make little dent in the image we emerge with after a nighttime's viewing, our enthusiasm long since tarnished by the shows which have come after, the commercials, the alarm clock waking us up the following morning to begin a new day.

Running Away: Vacations Which Never Last

6

Our job may not mean much, but there is always our two or three week vacation each year in which to recuperate, get ourselves back together, forget about it all. We rush home on the Friday our vacation is to start, gather the kids into the car already packed the night before, and drive madly six or eight hundred miles to a national park. On the way we have stopped at roadside restaurants, screamed at the kids to keep quiet and wait patiently for their food, to shut up and watch the scenery (though they never do). Sometimes we have driven into other campgrounds late at night only to find the spots taken, no place to pitch our tent or park our camper. Yet, we have finally gotten there, we and thousands of others, looking at the world's "most beautiful waterfall", the world's highest spire, the largest Ponderosa pine. A few days later we must begin the trek home.

Others of us will head for the airport for a trip to Hawaii, Bermuda, even Europe if we have the time and financial resources. Here we will eagerly gobble up new cultures, watch exotic dances, go to the world's oldest museum, visit a Roman church, a Greek Temple. Along the way we will buy native costumes, Dutch silverware, and talk to an average Norwegian in English. Loaded with stories and knickknacks we will head for home, exhausted but happy, having escaped our humdrum lives and found real adventure, if only for a short time.

Sound familiar? Vacations for many of us have become coping devices during which we seek to make up for forty-nine wasted weeks of work or thirty-six weeks of educational boredom. For many of us, such respites have become the central focus of the year, something to build toward, to prepare for in occupational and schooltime daydreams. It is often during our vacations that we hope to find our lost individualism, going where we want and doing what we want without having to worry about the consequences. In foreign lands who will know the difference, who will know how we really are "back home"?

Here, too, we would regain control over our lives, once again feel in charge, deciding where to stay, where to eat, what country to visit, what hike to take, which road to follow no matter where it may lead. Some of us take vacations to experience none of these things, simply to escape, or rest beside a cool pool, letting the ocean breezes soothe our tired minds and aching limbs. And still others go on vacation to put their marriages back together. *"On an idyllic island, honey, we'll be able to find each other again, to really relate, like we used to."* Despite what we might hope for, most vacations fall far short of our expectations, often leaving us as frustrated as when we left, returning to our "regular" lives still seeking fulfillment and salvation.

I

There are two broad avenues we would follow in trying to maximize our vacation possibilities. Taking the first route involves bringing our culture with us, taking what is familiar to us, and what already makes us feel comfortable and secure and transporting it to a new environment. The second route has us leave our culture and environment behind and immerse ourselves in a new culture, experiencing the adventure of a "new life" in another land.

There are many ways in which we take our culture and environment with us, both to insure our comfort and to make sure that nothing unexpected happens. The development of the recreational vehicle is a prime example of this kind of vacation. No longer do we have to leave for campgrounds and other parts of the nation unprepared. Campers are stocked with everything from gas stoves and refrigerators, color television sets and stereos, to water-beds. It is not uncommon in most campgrounds to see people huddled inside their "homes" watching the same television programs they might be viewing any other time of the year. What makes this a vacation is that no one has to get up and go to work or school in the morning, and one can still spend hours swimming in a lake or hiking up a nearby mountain. The best of both worlds — or is it?

Nor need one feel alone or uncomfortable in traveling across country. Nationwide chains of MacDonalds, Dennys, Ramada Inns, Best Westerns, and Holiday Inns await the weary traveler. Each is stocked with familiar items. Indeed, we can actually plot our trip by how many miles from one such establishment to the next – only thirty miles to your next Texaco station. Leaving the country, especially for the Continent, is little different. It is possible to go from Greece to Italy, to France, to England without leaving the United States. Chains of Hilton and Sheraton hotels assure the eager traveler that he or she can get the same hamburgers, banana splits, and even television programs regardless of where in the world we may be. And, on becoming frustrated even on these idyllic vacations, it is possible to adapt the same coping mechanisms as we might use back home in the states: television, consumerism, and alcoholism.

Unfortunately, most of us emerge from such vacations as dismayed as when we left, for not only do we take a good deal of baggage with us to insure our comfort, but we take a good amount of psychological baggage as well. If we spend forty-nine weeks living according to a specific time schedule, getting up at six-thirty each morning, rushing to work, then home, then to the television, how easy is it to alter such a schedule though we may be thousands of miles from our place of residence? Can we so easily shift gears and pretend we are somewhere else?

We also take many of our values with us. Used to justifying each minute spent even if it is allocated to watching television, it becomes quite difficult to just sit still, beneath a palm tree, coconut oil spread upon our skin. For those of us seeking more active vacations, we try not to waste a minute, attempting to get our money's worth out of every waking moment. As a result, we rush from this famous spot to that, a day in Paris, another in Rome, a third in Warsaw. Not wanting to take a chance that we will miss anything "important," or not wanting to chance the rigors of attempting to figure out another country on our own, we sign up for package tours which enable us to see ten countries in ten days. What a bargain. But what are we looking for? Why do we want to see that museum, or that church, or that statue, or that street? Most of us do not bother to ask these questions, so hurried are we that we barely have time to get off a quick snapshot in front of the Eiffel Tower.

The Protestant Work Ethic no longer realized on the job is readily translated to our vacations, as we attempt to consume other cultures without becoming a part of them. We go to tell others back home that we have been, that we have had the European Experience, and we have our photos to prove it. The camera, in fact, has become our portable television, insulating us from the actual event, taking the picture without having to be responsible for the content, without having to take part in anything we see, without becoming an actor on the "new land" stage. Click, and we change the channel. Like the Protestant Work Ethic, we feel guilty if we have not done our share, if we have missed something. What? You mean you didn't see the statue of David? Years later we can look back at our photo album and say, "Remember, Honey?" Remember what?

Nor do we view these monuments and cities as important centers of culture. Having little understanding of why we should be there — other than the fact that Travel Agency brochures and other travelers have told us to go — we have little idea what we have missed, though we know we have missed something. Most tourists congregate in places where other tourists are, herded into the Vatican with thousands of other camera-toting travelers, into an environment less made up of the paintings of Michelangelo than of the persons who would view his works, pushing and shoving to get a closer look. How little different than a subway ride in New York, or a freeway rush hour. How little we have escaped.

Even more important, we attempt to equate modern Italy with ancient Rome, modern Greece with the Parthenon. Instead of trying to relate to contemporary Italians, we spend all our time attempting to relate to their ancient ancestors, men having little relationship to their modern-day compatriots. Taking a picture of a statue, however, is easier than talking to a living Italian, but then what have we actually gained? How comfortable do we feel in surroundings little different from those we have left, spending the greater part of our time with persons little different from ourselves, and with the same tourist and "real life" problems? How much adventure do we find relating to stone monuments, using cameras as interpreters of our experience? Many of our domestic vacations are carried on in the same way. We travel from the midwest to the East to see the Capital, buy a miniature copy of the White House, eat at Der Wienerschnitzel.

Vacations must often be cloaked as learning experiences in order to justify the time and money invested in them. But how much learning has taken place in the kind of tourist trap atmosphere described above? Even more significant, however, vacations often take on the same consumerism mentality which we use to cope with occupational, relationship, and educational problems. Having experienced a new country means you have purchased something there. In Copenhagen and Amsterdam streets are blocked off, and whole sections of the city turned into small shops where tourists can browse and buy something culturally authentic. In this way we consume other cultures without having experienced them. Like the superfluous goods we purchase from our local shopping centers, our shelves are dotted with cultural artifacts we pay little attention to, and which bear little relationship to our day-to-day lives. To make our purchases easier, Bankamericard (Visa) and Master Card are accepted everywhere. Going camping in a national park means you return with a stuffed bear, a pennant, a dozen picture postcards. If we adapt the same attitude on vacation as we pursue in our daily lives, then what kind of vacation have we been on, where have we gone, how relaxed and renewed do we feel?

II

A second kind of vacation is more experiential in

nature. Here, we try and forget about our home environment and travel to other parts of the country or overseas in order to immerse ourselves in a different world. Unable to find adventure and excitement in our own society, we would seek it elsewhere, much as early adventurers sought out new, "undiscovered" lands. We might go to England and join a caravan which follows the route Marco Polo took overland to India. We might take up residence in Cuzco, Peru, learn the local language, and attempt to relate to the descendants of the Incas. We might journey to Tahiti, rent a thatched hut, and attempt to survive on the fish we pull in from a nearby lagoon. How "primitive" these cultures seem, how down to earth, how basic. They're not hung up on psychological problems, worried about whether their jobs are meaningful, about clothing and television. If we could only somehow be like them, then we too might be able to find our human "roots," discover who we really are. So we pack our bags and head for Cuzco for two months and from there attempt to make communication with mountain villages scattered in the surrounding valleys. But we discover that the mountain people do not trust us; they do not want our companionship, they do not want to accept us as members of their "family". Suspicious of our motives, they want us to buy things from them, or to leave them alone. Perhaps we have not made contact with the real "Indians," since the ones we have met appear to be tainted by Western civilization. We follow a narrow dirt road down a steep canyon by jeep, then go by canoe along a small river, till it opens onto a still larger body of water. We are on a tributary of the

Amazon. We hire a guide to take us into the "unknown," where the headhunters live, the people who paint their bodies and wear no clothing. It is two days' journey, he tells us. All the better, we reply. Soon we are there, motoring past a village, painted natives in loincloths standing on the bank, staring at us hostilely. This must be the real thing, we tell ourselves. We have finally arrived. The guide says we cannot stop because the natives are too dangerous. We agree, shooting pictures instead as our launch speeds out of range. Later we hear that the "headhunters" we have seen are paid by the guides to paint themselves and dress up as if they were still practicing the old ways. In a nearby town we think we recognize someone we saw standing on the bank several days ago. He is dressed in faded jeans, Disneyland t-shirt, and sandals. He does not smile when we pass him.

No matter how much we would like, there are no uncontaminated societies left. Western civilization has spread in rapid fashion around the globe, cutting down forests, setting up factories, selling transistor radios, bringing in technology and exporting local crafts. Just as we might wish to return to the Old West but find it impossible since it has disappeared, so too the existence of the "pure" native has also become a myth, perpetrated more in *National Geographic Magazine* photos, travel agency brochures, and in our imaginations, than in reality. The natives don't act like they're supposed to, because other tourists have come before, and often with far less noble intentions.

Yet, whether in fact untouched cultures exist and

are open for our inspection and involvement is one thing, a more serious issue is the question of whether or not we could ever become like them, accept their values, be a member of their "tribe". Despite romantic notions about living high in the Andes, life is extremely difficult even with exposure to Western civilization. Days are spent working vertical rows of crops which line the steep hillsides. One day a week is the long foot journey to market. There is no electricity, no running water, no toilets. How might we adjust to such a lifestyle? What would we do for entertainment? How do we erase our cultural heritage and background and open ourselves to the values of another people? We don't. After a short while, realizing that the people we are with are too different, or that they have already been "exposed," we take up the search again, hunting for another lost tribe.

Peoples of other lands can provide adventure, but it is frequently not the kind of adventure we are looking for, nor can such adventure help solve the problems we must face when we return home. Our society generates problems which reflect our level of technological development, the kind of economy we maintain, and the values it reflects. Other societies, particularly underdeveloped countries, have their own problems which typically have little to do with the way in which we articulate our own concerns.

This does not mean that there is not some relationship between their problems and ours, particularly if American economic interests are involved in exporting raw materials and finished products from these countries. But the personal identity crises, quality of work and education issues which plague our minds find little in common with the natives in whose values we would seek insight and solace. As a result, the adventure we experience is that of a tourist attempting to exist in a society he knows little about. The adventure lies in attempting to communicate, make friends, accept each other for who we are as representatives of the cultures we have emerged from, rather than attempting to "pass" as one of them. Such an experience can provide insight into how other peoples live, but it cannot enable us to solve our problems, any more than we can solve the problems they face by attempting to take on their cultural identity.

The best we can hope for, then, is a glimpse. But is this enough for our adventure-starved lives? Our time limited, we attend the festivals, go to the market towns, see natives on holiday, take pictures, read books about Indian lore and customs, buy native masks and sculpture, then go on to another village. We begin to find ourselves in the company of others on similar quests. People who have been everywhere, who have been on the road for two, maybe three years, restless, unable to settle down, to return home. These are the permanent tourists, the people without a country, free from having to deal with problems in any society, no longer responsible for what goes on around them because they are always visitors, always passing through, always outsiders. Yet, they are also homeless, without roots. While they have temporarily coped by escaping, in the long run it is no solution since the problems they run from do not go away, and since they are never accepted as citizens in the lands they journey to.

How different are they, though, from those of us who immerse ourselves in our television sets, tourists sitting in our living rooms watching and visiting the conflict and adventures played out before us on a picture tube? Tourists who daydream off during a classroom lecture, wishing we were somewhere else, someone else, a cattle baron or Indian chief. Tourists watching the evening news, events seemingly happening in another time and place. Tourists at the football stadium, and the movie theaters, and in the campgrounds watching the woods through the windows of our motor home, while the deer feed on bread crumbs we have left on a nearby table. Tourists because we cannot connect who we would like to be with who we are, or the society we would like to live in with the one we inhabit, and because we see no way of bridging the gap except through the fantasies held out before us by travel agents and television shows alike.

III

There is a third kind of vacation open to many of us. Instead of visiting another country, we visit ranches of the Old West, survive on our own or with a small group in a rugged wilderness in northern Canada, rent a cabin in the mountains and ski for two weeks, go fishing, take a five-day backpacking trip. Frustrated by passive jobs and sedentary lifestyles, we go off for awhile to find physical adventure, to put ourselves in tune with nature, to get away from the rat race. And we do. Our "city" problems are soon forgotten in the exhiliration of the hunt, the downhill slide, the feel of a horse beneath our overweight form. Our children, too, soon learn to forget about school as they go away to summer camp, sing folk songs, win merit badges. This is the good life, where problems are those of endurance, of physical aptitude and stamina. No foreign cultures to communicate with, no abstract problems of occupational alienation, meaningful relationships, smog, inflation. Simply build a campfire to keep warm and cook food, hike ten miles to the next destination, make it from the top of the ski run to the bottom without breaking a leg. Refreshing to know what you have to do, to be in control, to know it's all up to you with no one to tell you where you went wrong, or to block your progress, your sense of completion and fulfillment.

But then the vacation ends. Relaxed, refreshed and full of life, we return to our jobs, our schools, our dirty dishes and laundry. Yet there is nothing about our trip away from home, our adventure, which has enabled us to confront the problems we return to. Negotiating the difficulties of a ski run has little to do with organizing workers at our factory or in the office to deal with the emptiness and lack of fulfillment our jobs produce. Of course, this is not why we have gone on vacation. It is also why the power we feel in the mountain campsite cannot translate into power and control over our workplace, our classroom curriculum, or political power in American society.

Spectator Sports: Watching Your Favorite Team Win For You

7

Many of us are unable to get away for a two week backpacking trip. Either we feel physically inept, lack the financial resources, want to spend our vacation with our families, or are simply not motivated to expend so much energy. At the same time, we want some sense of adventure, of battles clearly won or lost in a world where nothing seems clear or final. A trip to a nearby football stadium on a Saturday or Sunday afternoon may be just what we are looking for. There, seated next to eighty or ninety thousand other stalwart fans, we can watch two teams do physical combat, much as the Romans some two thousand years ago cheered on their favorite gladiators.

Yet far from being passive spectators casually viewing twenty-two men push an oblong ball up and down a hundred yard grassy field, we find ourselves leaping to our feet, urging the defense to "kill'em", and loudly moaning as someone drops a pass in the end zone.

Throughout the contest, our heart races at three times its normal pace, our adrenalin pumping, as if we were on the playing field, as if we were making the key tackles, running the ball back after a kick-off, making an end run. For three hours we "lose ourselves" in the actions of sports heroes, deserting our humdrum lives for vicarious involvement with our athletic representatives.

While sports teams and their players can do little to solve our personal and social problems, it is indeed one of the ironies of American society that millions of men invest considerable energy keeping track of how well their team and its members are doing, even going so far as to hold certain players accountable for the actions they have taken in the name of their constituents. At the same time, no one pays attention to what their political representatives are doing, to the actions of those who would ostensibly take care of our pressing personal and social concerns. No one bothers to hold these persons accountable, to shout out encouragement when they rise against overwhelming odds to defend our position. Indeed, where is the **Sports Illustrated** of American politics, and if there is one, how many people subscribe?

I

Spectator sports are popular in American society because, for a minimal amount of effort, we can feel a part of the American dream. Free enterprise capitalism may no longer run the economy, but on the football playing field the individual can still "go all the way". There may be no new frontiers to conquer, but one team can still dominate another. Here too we see examples of individuals in control, guys with "take charge" attitudes, people who know what they want and go out and get it.

There are winners and losers, and everyone in the stands and sitting at home in front of their t.v. sets can readily identify who they are. Moreover, the losers have a chance to come back and be winners the following week. What could be more equitable than that? Hard work and discipline are also rewarded, as is physical prowess in a society geared almost totally to computerized calculations and "rational" decision making. It may be just a game, but it is one that is often far easier to get involved in than our jobs, classrooms, and relationships.

Professional sports teams also emphasize cooperation and team spirit, though more often than not, it is *individuals* who are selected out and rewarded while the efforts of their comrades, which might have made their "success" possible, are soon forgotten. A halfback may go through a hole in the line and run for a touchdown, and later, during a post-game interview, may comment on the fact that he could never have done it without the help of the other players who blocked out would-be tacklers; yet, the papers the next day will have little mention of this team effort. Sports announcers are also quick to point out a good block or tackle, but such efforts rarely make the evening news.

Yet while we may want to identify with sports heroes, dream of scoring touchdowns, making last-minute tackles, and clutch catches in the end zone, we usually cannot. First of all, we are not big enough, or fast enough, or skillful enough. Second, there are very few of them, which is why they receive so much attention, and millions of people like us. Nor, even granted the physical capabilities, are most of us willing to put out the energy necessary to be a pro star: there are too many other things we would rather do with our time. Wanting to see ourselves as sports heroes, but unable to actualize our wish, we must settle for being passive observers, sideline quarterbacks. While this role is often exhilirating, it is also frustrating and anxiety producing, for only our minds are on the playing fields. Our hyped up bodies and racing pulse jump frantically up and down in the stands, as a member of the opposing team gets loose and there is no one separating him from the goal line, but all we can do is tackle our t.v. set — we have no control over the events we see unfolding before us. This does little to alleviate our pent-up tensions; and indeed, many people die of coronary arrests in the stands, unable to vent their feelings.

Sports heroes also serve another purpose for men in American society. As more and more women come to occupy positions in the labor force, especially in middle management and professional positions, professional sports are seen as the last bulwark of masculine prerogative. By donning a football or baseball uniform, these athletes represent what it's like to still be a *real* man. The male spectator may feel insecure because women tell him what to do at work, or, at best, work alongside him, but at least in the stadium he does not have to worry about them infringing on his territory (unless, of course, the women in the stands with him also see these gladiators as real men and wonder why their boyfriend or husband cannot be like them).

Not only is living vicariously through a sports hero a coping mechanism for frustrations we feel powerless to deal with in our own lives, but sports teams themselves give us an identity we find more meaningful than our occupational status. Instead of saying, "I'm a bricklayer," or "I'm an insurance salesman," or "I'm at Lockheed", or General Motors, it becomes more significant and important to say: "I'm a Raider fan", or "I'm with the Mets". Seated in the stands with forty thousand other Raider or Jets fans we feel secure, a part of the effort, the spirit of camaraderie we are unable to find in other activities we may engage in. Even if we are home watching the game over our television sets, the post-game show in the locker room and the interviews with the players make us feel a part of the action, like "one of the boys". During halftime we can go out into the street and talk to our neighbors about the game, unless, of course, they are already in our family room watching with us. It also becomes easier to identify people, tell friend from foe by the name on their t-shirt and the bumper sticker on the back of their car.

Again, the fact that the team plays according to certan rules and norms which we can clearly label, and make sense out of, enables us to feel proud of our "membership" and equally of the team's accomplishments. This is a far cry from the ambiguity, fragmentation, and loss of purpose many of us experience on our jobs, in our school work, or even in our family life — though spending Saturday and Sunday afternoons in front of the set does little to make for family unity and cohesion.

It is not just football that builds this sense of identity, or has spectators label the professional participants as self-actualized Americans capable of realizing and living out the American dream. Baseball and basketball enforce the same allegiance, though in some ways reinforce other values as well. Particularly in the case of basketball, there is an air of craftsmanship which pervades the game. The ability to throw a round object over the head of an opposing player, while on the dead run, through a hoop twenty feet away, inspires the same awe and respect as did early painters, cabinet makers, and architects before the days when paintings, cabinets, and houses were mass produced. The labor we do might require little skill or talent, may in fact be an appendage to an automated assembly line or computer network, but on the basketball court, there are those who still take pride in what they do and in doing it well.

Not only may dad be a rabid fan, but child-rearing problems are often easier to deal with if kids want to follow in their father's footsteps. The family may not play together, but they can become spectators of the same games, Raider supporters alike. While most men cannot demonstrate to their kids what it's like to be an engineer, or dental equipment salesman, or assembly line worker, nor do they usually want to talk about their jobs after coming home from a difficult day at the office, they are more than willing to share their sports identities. It is relatively easy to talk about the rules of football or baseball, compare batting averages, or won-lost records. It's also easy to go out in the back yard or onto the street and throw the ball around. As male off-spring join Little League, their fathers can watch them "develop," see what kind of "men" (athletes) they will become. In a strange reversal of roles, many fathers who may not be active in playing sports themselves may give considerable encouragement to their sons to do so, often living through the deeds of their offspring much as they would vicariously identify with O.J. Simpson, Joe Na-math, or Bill Walton. For the father who has little interest in what his son is doing in school (his job) — since when he was that age he too had to endure the same kinds of classes and subject matter — it is a welcome relief to find solace in the coping device his son uses to avoid facing his problems. In this way too, lifestyle patterns are passed down from generation to generation, as fathers achieve immortality by leaving their athletic interest to their children. More often than not, however, these would-be heirs to the family "fortune" are unwilling to accept their inheritance. This results in a frustrated dad using all manner of mechanisms to push his reluctant child into becoming a superstar. *If you spend one more year playing football, I'll get you a car for your sixteenth birthday; if you don't, I'll never take you anywhere again.* Needless to say, such bribery rarely works, and if it does, only in the short run, as sons come to decide on their own how they want to spend their time. Nor do relationships of this nature make for a tight union between father and son, as the boy quickly grows frustrated at being unable to do what he wants, and in receiving little parental support for *his* interests, while his father becomes ever more impatient as he finds that his son does not live up to *his* expectations — win a college football scholarship, or make the Olympic team. Soon they stop communicating, lose respect for each other, and go their own ways.

II

Of course, for many reasons, athletics is good for people of all ages. It helps develop healthy bodies, can teach teamwork and cooperation. It's also easy to lose one-self in the competition, forget about other troubles as you swat handballs against a wall, feel the sweat pouring from your limbs, moving up and then back, breathing hard, your body responding automatically totally concentrating on the effort, on making a point. Of some concern, however, is the training young men and women receive in athletic competition. Kids learn more than just the rules of how to play baseball, basketball, and football. They learn disci-pline, and respect for authority, as well.

Yet, there is a fundamental difference between memorizing the rules someone else tells you are impor-tant, and coming up with these same rules on your own. School sports programs teach that there are certain ways of doing things, and if you want to play, you can only do so according to these regulations. While the junior high school coach may expect active bodies, he only requires a passive mind. Why aren't kids allowed to make up their own games, we might ask, games which reflect their immediate situation, which combine academic work and leisure activities? Why aren't they allowed to question why they only get to play baseball, basketball and football, and why they can only play by existing rules. The answer is not hard to come by. Kids cannot get involved in this kind of *re-creation* because it's not the way it's done, and because it might lead to other things.

If they question things like baseball and basketball rules, the next thing you know is they might begin to question the school curriculum — why do we have to talk about that today? And soon after the entire moral fabric of the country. On the other hand, if we can teach discipline and respect for authority on the playground, some of it may rub off in other areas of the child's life.

School sports programs also teach winning and losing. While most coaches say it's not, winning IS everything. If you win you get the trophy, if you play you get a letter that can be sewn on your sweater or jacket. Winning on the football field also becomes a ready substitute for not winning in the classroom, for not understanding what German history has to do with your life. It becomes a safe way of coping, one which society, dad, and others respect and support. It's also a way of letting off steam so that you don't have any energy left over to disrupt blackboard talks and homework assignments. The problem is that basketball trophies don't really mean very much when graduation time comes; unless you're especially talented, they don't help you get into college, nor do they enable the average student to connect his academic life to problems he may want to solve in his neighborhood, possible occupation, and family. It doesn't tell him how to gain power in society. The trophy is a way of buying him off. And what happens to those who play the game but get no trophies, no standing ovations, no victories? They become double losers, outcasts on the playing field, powerless in the classroom.

As the high school athlete is never taught to question the rules of the games he is playing, so too, the sports spectator never questions the values he would see actualized on the playing field before him. If competition no longer exists in the open market place, if individualism is gone from the supermarket and crowded freeways, why must we attempt to resurrect it in a football stadium or on a basketball court? Are these values still worthwhile? Why not substitute other values which better match the situations we now find ourselves in, values we don't have to be a sports hero to actualize or perform?

III

Sports can be a healthy activity, if we learn to develop our own games, or re-create those passed down from previous generations — if we do not stop participating and instead become spectators of others' accomplishments. School athletics can be beneficial as well, yet, as currently practiced they are a far cry from what is needed as adequate preparation for dealing with problems in other areas of our lives. The "pure" competition we would engage in on the basketball court does not match or prepare us for changing massive corporations and bureaucracies. Total involvement in athletic contests can sap energy which could be spent confronting personal and social problems. For the spectator who would immerse himself in the lives of professional sports heroes, *even if* football, basketball, hockey, and baseball games were played as microcosms of real life, were accurate reflections of the values and roles all of us attempted to live by, they would still fall short of the mark because we would still only be *watching*. Only *they* would be doing the playing. Never would it be our turn, because the nature of being a spectator does not prepare us for actual engagement. Rather, it encourages us to continue to be spectators, to let others take risks, receive the bruises of combat, while we sit high above them, cheering and drinking our beer. The grounding we come to feel as a fan is not real grounding, not based on our own actions and convictions; rather, it is an escape from having to confront the lack of such convictions, and the inability to find a place to practice them.

We may want to be sports heroes but we are, at base, assembly line workers, salesmen, English majors, and housewives. To the extent that we ignore these identities and the problems which are part and parcel of them, attempting to substitute athletic contests which have little bearing on how these identities are performed, to that extent we are coping. And the power we would feel from two football lines clashing can never be ours.

Love to the Rescue: Divorcing our Problems Away

8

One night you and your husband are invited to a party. After an hour or so you are introduced to a man you have not met before. His manner makes you laugh, and puts you at ease. He even looks a little like Robert Redford. How fresh and alive you suddenly feel! How far away the dinner dishes seem, the laundry, taking the kids to Scouts. You hardly even remember you're married. You glance over at your husband sitting on a couch across the room wolfing down chip and dip with one hand, a drink in the other, animatedly discussing some football game, his stomach protruding over his belt buckle, his hair noticeably thinning here and there. When was the last time he said anything interesting to you? When you really had a good conversation? When was the last time you felt attracted to him? How different this stranger seems, how refreshing. *It's too bad I'm married; too bad I'm not free.* A short time later the man you have just met asks you to meet him for lunch sometime. *"Why, ... I ... ,"* you reply, startled, blushing, flattered;

". . . maybe . . . sometime."

Romantic love has become a way of coping with unsatisfactory marriages without giving up our marital vows. It has also become a lifestyle for many single people looking for the perfect mate as well as for those who view playing the field as a worthwhile goal in its own right. For this last group, it is the process of *falling* in love that is important, not whether we actually settle down or end up with any one person. There are so many interesting and attractive people in the world to "get it on with," or so the rationale goes, why hold back, why not hit as many bars and parties and bedrooms as you can? How "together" we feel sitting at a table in our favorite night spot when someone at the next table says "Oh, excuse me," and we get to talking, and the next thing we know we're back at the apartment. The candles are already lit around the waterbed, reflecting off the satin sheets. We duck into the bathroom to put on a final dab of cologne, and then she excuses herself. Two more glasses of wine, and then — did she have an orgasm (I wonder if he thinks I'm good), oh well — our eyes closed, falling asleep, not saying anything to each other in the morning as we drop her off, we'll be in touch, okay?

How easy, and empty.

I

Romantic love got its start somewhere around the 13th century, when relationships were carried on between knights in shining armor and ladies of the court, both of whom were typically married to someone else. The idea was that passion was heightened if consummation was never achieved, that is, if the respective partners never ended up in bed together. Romance came to symbolize courtship: flowers, poems, gifts, long glances from afar. Once having slept together, however, the game ended, and a new love had to be found. This conception of love corresponded nicely to the notion of having a virgin bride which personified dating in American society until the mid-sixties. With the development and widespread acceptance of birth control pills, as well as other forms of contraception, however, attitudes toward sex began to change.

The general quesioning of traditional ways of doing · things by the "counter culture" also gave encouragement to the belief that sex should be enjoyed for its own sake, and need not be limited to marital partners, or couples who were engaged. Yet, if consummation can be achieved on the first date, what then happens to the romance? What is there to keep the man enticed, and at the same time give the woman a sense of power in the relationship? If she doesn't hold out, then what other kind of leverage does she enjoy? Ideally, as sex becomes a normal part of relationships, couples will find other things to decide their compatiblity upon: similar interests, complementary personalities, mutual support and affection. In many cases, this is in fact what happens and romantic love is enlarged to encompass a deep daring for one another. In countless others, however, romance takes on a far different character.

The romantic ideal is translated from an attempt to seduce one person, to seducing as many as possible in our search for a "perfect love" or "soulmate". The inability to find complete satisfaction with one person confirms the need to continue the search, and after awhile, the search becomes everything for our perfect love may be only a mental construct, a fantasy. Caught up in the pursuit of romantic love, we are not allowed to stop and consider whether or not our idealized image exists in reality, for to do so would be to end the game and to discredit the coping mechanism we would successfully employ.

Many of the values Americans pay lip service to serve to guarantee that consummation can never be achieved, that satisfaction will be difficult, and that we will never find the one we are looking for. Being single and on the make is one of our few opportunities to be individualists. We may go out with lots of people and bed them as well, but where does it say that we have to *relate* to them, compromise our values if need be, and adjust to their expectations? After all, we are in search of our one and only, and when we find them, the perfection we will experience together will enable us to be true to ourselves, do whatever we want whenever we want, because they will love us for who we are. Yet, in our "real life world," unable to give anything up, to see ourselves as part of a twosome, we make sure that the unity we want to experience never takes place.

Not only do we tend to see ourselves as romantic individualists, but such individualism is based on a free enterprise open marketplace conception of freedom. In our quest, we are free to see as many people as we like. Being only responsible for ourselves and our actions, we never have to worry about who gets hurt along the way. Go out with someone, drop them, go out with someone else, drop them also, what difference does it make, when it is OUR individuality, and OUR needs that are most important? Yet, the free spirits many of us picture ourselves to be are, in actuality, victims of our own imagination. The freedom we see ourselves having is contingent on the willingness of others to go along with what *we* want to do, contingent on other people sharing dinner and bed with us. Nor is it freedom to give up the search, to stop hustling, to put our energies else-where. Yet, seeing ourselves as free agents allows us to be in control, to be independent, because in not having to relate to anyone, to share ourselves, we also do not have to submit to decisions others may make about our lives. We may control nobody but ourselves, but that is better than being powerless to all. Afraid of giving up this last shred of "security" and, as we see it, meaningful identity, we seek ways of making ourselves invulnerable. We refuse to divulge our real feelings, to trust anyone, to cry. We hide behind an array of pre-conceived "lines", humorous stories, and episodes we communicate. There, secure behind our mask, we watch, and wait for our loved one to appear; free, so long as we do not let go, do not become involved and dependent. And, if we do, picking up and moving on.

One of the ways in which romantic involvements are

played out is according to certain standards of beauty. Coincidentally, these same standards are portrayed in movies, television commercials, novels, and children's dolls. The more beautiful we are, the greater our freedom because then more people will feel attracted to us and want to go out with us (take us to bed). The better looking we are, the less we have to compromise, and the more power we have because we have more choice, and are therefore less dependent on any one person. If we were not born beautiful, we need not spend an inordinate amount of time worried about this fact, because our economy abounds with ways of helping us out. Cosmetics industries, fat farms, clothing manufacturers all do their share and are more than willing and able to act as a support system for our would-be identity.

Unfortunately, the focus on beauty has not made for better relationships, it has only insured that consummation and fulfillment are not achieved. A relationship based on physical appearance alone leaves a couple with little else to do but make love, an admittedly worthwhile activity, but one that is insufficient to maintain mutual interest since there is always someone potentially more beautiful waiting in the wings. Besides, what are we going to say to each other over dinner? Moreover, beauty in and of itself does not insure growth and process in a relationship; rather, it is a passive characteristic. One is either beautiful or one is not, even with cosmetic aids, and there is little more that can be done. One only grows beautiful if beauty is considered as the sum expression of one's existence, a reflection of one's personality, rather than the physical structure within which this personality is housed. Nor are those considered beautiful "free," for they are constantly *dependent* on verification by others, on compliments and attention. It is no accident then, that often the most "beautiful" of people are also the most insecure, because they can never rest on their laurels.

And what happens to those who cannot compete? Those whom no amount of cosmetics can make attractive by motion picture standards of appearance, or those once blessed, but who now find age creeping over them? Face-lifts for the wealthy; how do the others cope? Perhaps they find better ways of establishing relationships.

Romantic love has become the new consumerism, but like all attempts to objectify and treat the product as an end or solution in itself, it does not work. Romantic love as a total lifestyle becomes a way of coping with lack of identity, purpose and meaning in other areas of our lives. Escape into fantasy is easy as we daydream off about our potential evening conquest, while another pile of forms to fill out is placed on the desk before us. Songs on the radio attest to our victories and losses, and we hum along accordingly. Life is a dance, providing we stay in tune, and out of the way of the real power brokers, the corporations, schools, and politicans which employ us and have us do their bidding. The pursuit of romantic love keeps us isolated and insecure, always wondering how well we are doing, have they published the new ratings? It also keeps us powerless, focused on an object we can never achieve, alternately frustrated by our inability to find perfect love and satiated by our temporary victories, our mouth-to-mouth resuscitation and orgasms. In the meantime, our attention is diverted from other problems we face and with which we must deal, problems which must be solved before we can hope to engage in any satisfactory relationship. For we cannot be "free lovers" while being assembly line slaves, divorce our sexual capitalism from the corporate monopolies which employ us, be individualists in the bedroom and powerless robots on the freeways of America.

II

Many of us soon grow tired of looking for a perfect love. Still others of us were never looking in the first place, but rather became romantically involved with someone whom we got along with, and settled down with them, trying to accept their bad qualities as well as their good ones. Soon after moving in together, we begin to notice problems. She doesn't seem interested in sports. All he ever wants to talk about is what happened on *his* job or *his* friends; I might as well be the couch in the living room for all the attention I get. She doesn't look the same anymore, and look at the weight she's beginning to put on, those lines under her eyes. How come she doesn't like to go skiing? Why doesn't he help with the dishes or the laundry, Christ, it's *his* underwear . . . Different sources of discontent begin to develop. We begin to feel something missing, but can't quite put our finger on it. There's nothing to look forward to. We've settled into a routine and can't seem to break it; it's too easy to stay just the way we are, too comfortable just to let things ride, turn on the television . . .

117

besides, she's got her interests and I've got mine. Maybe we should have a kid, that would bring us back together, give us something in common.

Living together and marital vows have become a significant form of coping for a large number of people in American society. Like our chase after perfect love, we expect our marriage to make a difference in our lives. If we are living with someone, then all of our other problems will magically disappear. Unable to confront problems at work, in school, on crowded freeways, we put all our energy into our marriage in the hope that it can "save" us, protect us from oblivion. Yet, no one person can satisfy all of our needs, nor was the marital institution designed to do so. An identity lost at work cannot be replaced by one established in the home. The worthlessness and frustrations we feel from a day at the office cannot be adequately dealt with by talking them over with our wife or husband, or more often than not by taking them out on them, because it was not in our marital relationship that these problems developed in the first place. Unable to find meaning in other areas of our lives, we put excessive pressure on our family relationship to fill the void, but it cannot. As a result, we begin to grow dissatisfied, blaming our relationship instead of our job for our lack of happiness. Totally dependent on our wife or husband to give our lives purpose and meaning, we grow insecure, easily threatened, jealous and possessive, worried that they might find someone else, and then we would have nothing. The more worried we become, the more conflicts develop in our relationship as we come to question every frown, ask them why they were late coming home, study their interaction with "friends". For those of us who have married or moved in with someone on the basis of their physical appearance, (the beauty described earlier), reliance on this relationship to satisfy all of our needs is a shattering experience indeed. What can such a relationship give us, how can it possibly cope with the myriad of problems we face and would find solace for?

Instead of supplying the security, control and power we so desperately need, we find that marriage too is just one more area of our lives that has let us down. Yet, where else can we go? This was our last chance. At first we attempt to rationalize our situation. Our relationship isn't so bad, afterall, why, look at the Harris's. They're always screaming at each other; at least we don't do that. Besides, it's nice to come home to a good meal and watch the kids play in the back yard. What else could we do, anyhow? Soon, our rationalization turns to resignation. That's just the way marriage is.

For many of us, coping with a marriage that doesn't meet our expectations means blaming our partner for our lack of satisfaction. If I hadn't married him, why I'd have my own advertising agency by now. If I hadn't been such a smuck, I could have really gone somewhere. It also means, in many instances, turning our attention outside the relationship to the possibility that another partner might better fulfill our needs. "God," you say, while watching an afternoon soap opera one day, "if I had only married someone like that, I'd never be in the fix I'm in now," or, following the cult of beauty, you look longingly at a woman across the aisle in the supermarket, "if I could be with her, I'd never be sorry."

It doesn't take much time before we begin to consider whether we might be able to have our cake and eat it too. We meet someone at a party and arrange to see them for lunch. One day we stay late at the office. For many of us, however, there are only mental affairs. I wonder what he'd be like? For us, there is no risk involved, no guilt, because we never really find out. Seeing someone on the sly once a week, twice a month for a couple of hours helps relieve the tension at home, we rationalize, as our guilt has us do the dishes, fix his favorite dinner, take her to a show she has been wanting to see. Perhaps the family isn't so bad after all, we reason. Yet, we find it difficult to avoid the comparison, the wife at home, her hair in curlers, our lady friend always dressed up, always perfumed, problem-free. Since we see them so infrequently, we never grow tired or lose our attraction. They represent the perfect love image we have been searching for, the one the magazines and television, movies and ads are always tempting us with. And if they are not the one, then there are always others. It is as good a way of coping as any. We never have to deal with problems in our marriage, because these problems don't really "bother" us anymore; we no longer pay attention to them. We can have the security of our family, while at the same time, put adventure back into our lives, become the dashing and romantic figures we always dreamed of being. And, the better we are able to pull it off, the more our status goes up among our friends who "know" our secret, and some friends have to know to make it worthwhile.

By breaking a societal taboo, we again become individualists, independent creatures who once more are in control of their lives. Yet, since our marital problems remain, as well as those issues external to our marriage (our alienating jobs), having an affair does not substantially alter the state of our lives. Nor are most affairs ultimately very satisfactory. It is difficult to manage a balance between being in two places at once, always having to cover our tracks. It takes time and energy. Often the constant lying begins to gnaw at our system, making us tense and irritable no matter where we are. Afraid of getting caught, our actions often become more deliberate and easy to figure out. The other woman or man begin to want to see us more frequently, begin to make demands, especially if they have no one else to go home to, or are looking for a more permanent kind of relationship. We too begin to wonder what a more lasting relationship would be like with them, how carefree. Yet, as long as we are never with them totally, we can preserve our romanticism and our daydreams, never having to run the risk that we were wrong. On the other hand, not being able to see them whenever we like makes us frustrated and irritable, out of control again, powerless because we may never know, and because it is possible that we may miss our one chance for salvation.

For some of us, the conflict becomes overbearing, affecting all aspects of our lives. Say, what's gotten into Harry lately? Have you seen Ann, why she looks terrible. This in turn leads us into having to make a fundamental choice: stay with our family, or go elsewhere. Giving up our outside involvements means telling ourselves it wouldn't have worked, anyway—everyone knows that all living together arrangements are the same. Leaving our family means starting over, either with someone we are already carrying on with, or a still as yet unknown lover. We weigh the odds. We're not getting any younger, the old beer belly, the thinning hair, maybe we should count our blessings and stay where we are. But this may be our last hope; Jesus, another thirty years of life with him. We make a break for it, separate from our family, throw him out, start over.

It is rarely a clean break, especially if there are children involved. We move in with someone else, but they don't understand our children, even if the children are only up on weekends. The guilt we may feel for abandoning our offspring begins to cloud our new relationship as we look for a channel for our increasing frustrations. The woman stuck at home with two kids has a hard time attractng a new man who must consider the additional burden her children present. Then too, her children are always there to remind him of the missing husband, their father. And where do you meet someone else, anyhow? What do you say to them? It's been so many years. We attempt to make ourselves beautiful, attractive, eligible; gear ourselves up for competing with men and women ten years our junior, falling back on what "worked" in the past, not knowing anything else to do. After a series of one night stands, we readjust our standards. Having become lonely and desperate, we are willing to settle for anyone who will help us deal with our isolation. Yet, once having done so, how much less able our new relationship is when it comes to satisfying all of our needs. Perhaps, though, we do meet someone we really like, but having never dealt with the crux of our marital problem, what is to prevent the same mistakes from occurring? What is to prevent this relationship from being like our last, no matter how good it seems in the beginning, since we have not solved any of our other problems and as a result are still totally dependent on our relationship to give our lives meaning?

While divorce may be a legitimate solution for many marriages confronted with irreconcilable differences, it may also be an escape. Once having blamed our first marital partner for our other problems, how easy it becomes to do so again. Divorce may indicate something else as well, however. In many cases it represents our inability to face conflicts, our unwillingness to hassle through problems which can be solved no better in another living together situation. And yet, where have we learned to solve such problems—in our public schools? on television? at work? Divorce becomes the solution to those of us who have adapted coping as our dominant lifestyle. For the couple not tied by a marriage license, the tendency to split when the going gets tough is even more pronounced, for here there is no community property to worry about, no kids, no divorce settlement and legal problems to work through. In fact, it is often the piece of paper that means so little, that keeps many couples struggling to stick together, often with mixed results.

III

Sometimes we are not alone in trying to decide our marital future, for it is the rare couple who separates or gets a divorce without first consulting a marriage counselor. What is curious is how marriage counselors typically define marital problems. First you each see the counselor individually. Perhaps there is a communication problem, the counselor suggests. You don't tell each other what you want out of the relationship. You're just not in love anymore you say to her; he doesn't give a damn about me, she replies. The counselor has you try various communication experiments, maybe get away for a weekend alone without the kids to interfere. Look at all the years you've invested, don't you think you should try one more time? the counselor asks. But you *have been* communicating, you tell her; there's just nothing more to say, we know each other *too* well. We can almost read each other's minds. Maybe you should try fighting more, the counselor advises. But about what? we both answer in unison.

Marital counselors may help when there is indeed a communication problem, but even here, once we have said our piece, there is no guarantee that we will like what we hear, or that it will make for a better relationship. But marriage counselors fail on more serious grounds. They see all marital problems as lying *within* the marriage relationship; the solution then must somehow entail either changing marital patterns or changing the attitude of each individual partner. Nowhere do marriage counselors attempt to examine marital problems as symptomatic of problems occurring in American society in general, and in the roles we play outside our marital relationship in particular. Frustrations are seen as developing within the marital framework, not because we are pissed about the way we are treated at work, or because we cannot understand why our heavy consumer purchases have not brought satisfaction and fulfillment. If the blame were shifted to where it is due, then marriage counselors would be community organizers, getting us to band together with other families to fight back against the problems that trouble us, and to do so in the jurisdictions in which they occur.

But marriage counselors do not see the family as a political unit, as a microcosm of the values, structure and problems of the larger society, nor do family members themselves. On the contrary, by defining the family as a separate entity, it becomes impossible to resolve many of the problems family members face, particularly conflicts between husbands and wives. It also means that a marital union will never be seen as a launching pad from which to attack problems we face in other areas of our lives. Rather, our energies invested in maintaining our territory against intrusion by other couples, or single people on the make, we grow ever more isolated and alone, powerless to see our way clear of the trap that has ensnared us.

I'M Okay, Who Cares How Everyone Else Is Doing

9

Oftentimes we are forced to adapt a particular coping behavior not only because we cannot face problems at work or school, but because our other coping mechanisms have failed us. We find ourselves dreaming off during an episode of CHIPs, bored by the same plot, feeling anxious and restless while another criminal is apprehended. As we wash and wax our new car, our hands merely go through the motions, no longer able to take pride in ownership, to feel good about who we are when we're in the driver's seat. We take our weekly trip to a nearby shopping center, but cannot find anything to buy, nothing seems to fit right, we give up in frustration. Our team wins, but the victory seems hollow; unable to be on the playing field, we feel ourselves withdrawing, despite the wildly cheering fans around us. Your husband says: maybe we should get away for awhile, Hawaii, Mexico; sure, why not, you reply half-heartedly, visions of poolside boredom restlessly stirring in your cranial cavity. I wonder if there's something the matter with me, you begin to ask yourself.

On the recommendation of a friend we pay a visit to a clinician, a psychotherapist who has an office in a nearby medical complex. We sit on a comfortable couch, attempting to respond to his inquiries. When did we first start feeling this way? We tell him briefly about our childhood, the time mother spanked us for eating too many cookies, the time our parents fought late into the night, how brother Tom never liked us. And now? he asks. We tell him how alienated we feel at work, how distant real life seems, how many of our friends lie to us, how the large mortgage payment we must dole out each month and the house that goes with it does not seem worth it, how we are living in a neighborhood where no one talks to anyone else, and with a spouse and kids who rarely speak to each other except during television commercials. As a result we feel stressful and anxious and cannot sleep at night. We go back to our past again. Did we love our mother? Was father too authoritarian? What kind of dreams have we been having? Snakes? Oceans? A car accident? Our therapist might suggest that we seem to have trouble communicating, being open and honest about our real feelings. How about enrolling in an encounter group where you can get direct feedback about how others actually see you? We take their advice and join the encounter group where, at the first session, we tell the group about our family, job, the drive to work and back on the freeway, the boredom of NBC week, the neighbors. The group members respond. Someone says he thinks we're blocking; another adds that the problems we mention don't seem on target, something is missing, we're not happy with ourselves; we don't trust anyone; we don't know who we really are. We're not assuming responsibility for our lives. Later in the evening we all hold hands, sitting in a circle with our eyes closed; then we hug each other one by one as we leave.

The next morning one of the kids throws a bowl of cold cereal at his sister, we automatically kiss our spouse goodbye, the freeway jams at the usual point, the same stack of papers lies on our desk at work. Perhaps the source of our problem does not reside in our head as much as in the society in which we live.

I

For every person in a mental hospital there are perhaps thousands who pay weekly visits to psychological therapists of one bent or another. Some go because they need someone to talk to and cannot trust any of their friends. Others go because they feel their lives empty and worthless, and still others because therapy is considered the only legitimate way of dealing with their "personal problems." Therapy is an attractive alternative because, conceptually speaking, it does not necessitate a change in our basic value framework. While going to a therapist does mean admitting that we cannot face our problems or cope on our own, the manner in which therapy is practiced typically shifts the burden back onto our own shoulders, holding us responsible for any cure that may be forthcoming. Moreover, the heart of psychological therapy is that the problem lies with us, not with the society in which we live. As a result, any problem we may broach to our therapist or encounter group is seen as an individual matter, a personal problem whose solution lies in changing our own attitude, rather than worrying about changing the environment around us, in which the root causes of our problem may lie.

The message behind psychological therapy is that if we get our own head together, the rest will take care of itself. But is this really true? Is psychological or self-help therapy a way of enabling us to confront our problems, or simply another coping mechanism many of us use to make our lives easier to deal with, more comfortable and acceptable?

One of the central concepts of self-help therapy is that we really don't understand who we are. Rather, we have masked ourselves behind a cover-up of roles and disguises which make us play phony games. In order to get in touch with our *real* selves, we must discard the rational world in which we have been raised and by which we conduct our lives, and get in touch with our feelings. This is done in a variety of ways. Some therapists attempt to get us to go back to our childhood, re-experiencing a particularly emotional trauma which comes out in the form of a "primal scream," thereby reawakening our deeper emotional selves. Another, more positive version of this is to get us to have a "peak" experience, mentally recreating one of our favorite memories or fantasies. Here again, once having gotten in touch with our buried feelings, we can allow them to become a part of our everyday world. We relax in a chair, our eyes closed, while the therapist takes us back, you were walking along a stream, touching his hand, the water murmured quietly beside you, through you . . .

It is felt that our feelings are more honest than our explanations of our feelings; that our emotions tell us more about the problems we are experiencing than any rational description. In some cases this may be true, yet our feelings are often reflections of our reasoning processes. We feel badly because we have not matched the expectations of the society in which we live, we have not made it to the top of our class, we do not hold an executive position, and to the contrary, have not been promoted in ten years. Our wife does not match the beautiful lady we see on a perfume advertisement. Getting our feelings out may help describe our attitudes, but it will not alter the societal expectations we are responding to. Yet, that isn't a problem because psychological therapy does not want us to alter these expectations; rather, it seeks to make us comfortable in our own successes, however limited these may be. I'm okay just the way I am.

Understanding who we are, does not mean understanding ourselves in terms of environmental pollution, occupational alienation, or the corporate profit system. Rather, it means somehow mentally separating ourselves off from their influence and existing in a world strictly of our own making. Contrary to all the literature demonstrating that we are social beings, dependent on other people for support and affection, self-help therapy has us see ourselves as "our own best friend." Seemingly, if we don't have to worry about anyone else, then we can do whatever we want, providing, of course, we stay within the confines of our own heads. How similar this is to other coping devices we have attempted. Again we find ourselves in control, feel powerful, because there is no one who can challenge that power; indeed, no one else knows about it, since it does not seek public expression in challenging private coporations and public bureaucracies. The power exists in the secret smile we maintain—I know something you don't know. Armed with our new self-knowledge, we can insulate ourselves from the damaging impact of superficial relationships, corporate ads, freeway traffic jams, and boring jobs. At the same time, we also insulate ourselves from ever having to do anything about these problems. We can be who we are without having to risk anything, or put anything on the line. Nor do we ever have to compromise our individuality. Taking charge in self-help therapy terms, then, means assuming responsibility for who we are, providing the "who we are" is limited to how we see ourselves and not how others see us, and providing the "who we are" is not determined by the occupations we engage in, the cars we drive, and the relationships we enter into along the way.

As Edwin Schur points out in a book entitled *The Awareness Trap*, most therapy of this kind comes to be about *techniques* or *processes* for understanding oneself, the methods of self-knowledge, rather than the knowledge itself. In some ways this is similar to the way elementary school children are taught, focusing on the three R's, rather than the subject matter which these learning methodologies help us to understand. In encounter groups, people are told that open and honest communication will solve their problems. Yet, as we noted in the last chapter, is communication enough? What if we have nothing to say? What if we have little comprehension of how our feelings relate to our actual situation in American society, how than does communication help us to solve our dilemmas, let alone enable us to get in touch with ourselves? Communication without effective analysis of what is taking place is communication without solution. Yet, to put content into therapy would be to force individuals to take a stand vis-a-vis the society in which they live. Being honest with ourselves would force us to confront those societal values and institutions which alienate us. So much easier not to. In fact, one of the major attractions of therapy is that it does not necessitate a change in personal lifestyle. One doesn't have to give up his house in the suburbs, change jobs or transform his occupational workplace, because the problem is not seen as lying in any of these areas. One simply has to change his attitude, learn to let out his feelings, adapt a more acceptable rationale for his self in the world. At the same time, we remain powerless to do anything about problems which continue to crop up. Content in our own individualism, we continue to be isolated and alone, unable to see our problems as social in character, and consequently, unable to organize with others to do something about them. Yet, since our therapy has given us a way of approaching life, rather than a meaningful rationale on which to base our existence, something which we can be honest and open and relating about, and since other people, and the society in which we must live, frequently do not share our view of the world and of ourselves, we must continue to return to our therapist or encounter group for reinforcement and encouragement. Or, if the guide words they have given us no longer seem to fit, we can try some new form of therapy, one which *really* gets our feelings out. Since the root causes of our personal problems have not been dealt with, it is not unusual for many people to spend years in one kind of counseling or another without finding any appreciable change in their lives. Is this any different than the consumer who, on discovering that one cosmetic has not done the job, not attracted the men it was supposed to, switches brands in hopes of deliverance, without the realization that the process of consumerism itself may be the reason for their failure? Not very many therapists are worried about the return rate of their patients, or that their clients do not seem to be getting anywhere, for, among other things, if clients solve their problems, therapists would be out of a job. And then, who would pay *their* Bankamericard bills?

To many of us, therapy takes too long, or is too expensive. Thirty-five to forty dollars an hour is a lot to pay one day a week for three years. Nor, are many of us willing to expose ourselves to the "honesty" of fellow citizens as expressed through encounter group sessions. Why go through the hassle? Besides, if we are responsible for our own solution then that solution lies with the individual, rather than with the group. Why not cut out the middle man, especially when we are attempting to avoid conflict rather than confront it? Self-help therapy books become an obvious solution. They are cheap and practical, enabling us to take our therapist with us. This also saves time. When we must grab for the gusto, and live in the here and now, lengthy therapy sessions can prove frustrating. A quick look at any drugstore bookrack, or the psychology section of any bookstore, will reveal a myriad of self-help therapy titles, many of which are remakes of the theory of positive thinking. Many include step-my-step guides to tell how well we're doing, procedures to follow for any situation we might find ourselves in. If in doubt, we can simply say, wait a minute, and look up the approporiate response. Body language books are particularly germane as one learns how to manipulate others and get what he wants, by giving off subtle cues.

Nor are other kinds of therapy practiced without a moral or manipulative message, even when put into use with the guidance of a counselor. Being open and honest can often be used in a destructive as well as constructive manner. The pursuit of self-interest goals, so that we can maximize our own potential, is often done at the expense of other persons who may not agree with what we are doing. But that's all right, because they're *not okay,* there's something the matter with them which they'd better "get together". Such self-actualization is often interpreted to mean that we are "free" to do whatever we want in the name of getting in touch with ourselves and finding out who we really are.

Yet, if we can determine our own moral code, then so too can others: there is no necessity that we agree, since we live in a world where each of us must find his own way, according to his own dictates. Despite what many therapists claim, such democratization does not lead to a more humane society, a world in which everyone wins;

rather, it leads to the capitalistic ethic of I-win, you-lose which many of us have been raised on. Indeed, the very term "self-actualization" belies the self-interest character of psychological therapy. If we were really interested in a more humane world, then shouldn't the guide word for our efforts be more logically called *social actualization:* everyone-wins or no one finds satisfaction and fulfillment.

The I-win, you-lose philosophy underlying self-help therapy reinforces our neglected individualism; it also gives us a new status. Not only do we have a secret guide to success, but we have also been through something others have not. We have been initiated into a group whose souls have been saved; we are more "aware" than anyone else. Our status, however, is typically only good within encounter group and therapy circles. Accordingly, those who have been through many years of therapy, or several encounter sessions, come to feel that they are more honest than newcomers, more open and feeling. Yet, in order to maintain their status, they must continue to encounter, continue to engage in therapy, for once outside their chosen preoccupation, few would recognize the symbols on which they would base their new-found prestige.

In the last few years, the language of self-help therapy and encountering has spread far beyond the jurisdiction of the saved. As R.D. Rosen has pointed out in his book Psychobabble, the cliches of the therapy movement can be glimpsed everywhere. I can really *relate* to what you're saying. I *hear* you, baby. I can really get *in touch* with that.

In an interesting and often sad way, the proliferation

of self-help therapy jargon has lessened the status of those who would claim such language as a part of their own distinct culture. If "everyone" is in "touch" and "really relating", then who is to know who the true followers really are? If they really HEAR what you're saying. In another sense, however, since therapy status symbols have no relationship to power in the real social world, that is, power to solve personal and social problems, then such a status can never have very much on which to stand.

II

For some of us, self-help therapy takes the form of meditation and the seeking after a higher consciousness. We come home from a difficult day at work, take off our shoes, and sit cross-legged on the floor in our bedroom, ignoring the sounds and smells emerging from the kitchen, the kids fighting in the family room, the television. We may do breathing exercises to help us relax, or muscle tensioners. The outside world gradually disappears, we are alone in ourselves, the rhythm of our heart beat. Soon, our individual self drops away, and we are at one with the universe, the underlying pulse of life. Here, physical form no longer matters, we have become part of the collective unconscious which fills all cells, all matter. Here too, past and future lives merge, perhaps we were once a butterfly, or a redwood tree, a thirteenth century serf, or a water buffalo.

Today we live in the suburbs, work in a bank;

tomorrow, in the life after this one, we may be a gardener, or a rock. As we come to view our immediate world as transitory, problems in it seem mundane, not worth hassling with. After all, they are merely shadows on the cave, apparitions having no relationship to our real essence. What difference does it make if we solve these problems, if work is alienating, since alienation is only a surface manifestation of the real meaning of existence?

For many of those who partake of the higher consciousness, who follow this Maharishi or that, even traditional forms of self-help therapy are seen as fruitless gestures, since they acknowledge the cult of individualism. The higher consciousness transcends individualism; it also transcends society. Nor is the universe, or the manner in which the universe is organized, seen as the problem, because the universe is the universe — there is no cause and effect, no moral judgment — the universe is a process unfolding, and we are a part of it; there is nothing we can do, one way or the other, to change its course.

For those well practiced in the art, meditation of this kind becomes an ideal coping mechanism. We don't have to worry about our problems, because those problems are only temporary, they will go away in another lifetime or two. We can do whatever we like without feeling guilt, without worrying about whether we have made the correct decision, since all decisions are the right ones, and indeed, the only ones we could have possibly made. While we have given up any claim to control over our destiny, our powerlessness does not bother us, because the notion of power itself is a "false" concept.

Unfortunately or fortunately, depending on our perspective, most of us in the United States have a difficult time carrying meditation this far. For us, it becomes a way of relaxing or "centering" ourselves, a way of regrouping our energies. Brought up in a cause and effect society, where time, individualism and power are important, we can only relinquish such concepts temporarily, and only then when we are not besieged by our other problems. At best, then, meditation becomes a temporary escape, a means of gaining some perspective on a problem in which we have invested too much or taken too seriously Yet, since its underlying principles do not provide a way of dealing directly with our problems, or even defining them as important, meditation cannot show us how to solve them.

III

A similar form of fatalistic "therapy", though one which is more oriented toward worldly concerns, is made up of astrological predictions, Tarot, and the I Ching. Like meditation, we are not considered responsible for our problems, since these problems are determined by other things, not society, but the moon and the stars and other elements. How we act each day, astrologically speaking, is determined by what sign we are – a Libra, Taurus, Aquarius – or, when further delineated – a Libra rising or falling, a water or air sign, and the exact hour on which we were born. For a small sum, we can have our fortunes told. Will she marry me? Will I fall in love again? When will I die? Will my trip be a good one? Reading Tarot cards helps supply similar answers. As each card is picked, the picture on it tells a story, helps us interpret the direction our life is to take, what problems we may encounter and how these will be resolved. And so too with the I Ching.

What each of these techniques provides is an attempt to give us insight into ourselves without holding us responsible for what happens to us. Again, however, no one is responsible, nor does the way in which our society is organized, or its values, determine our behavior. There is nothing we can do but hang in there, and read our astrological prediction every morning in the paper. Powerless, we let the reading become a self-fulfilling prophecy, as we spend the day looking for those things that seem to lend support to what it has told us. Yet, instead of enabling us to face our problems, the messages which appear in our reading are of such a general nature as to fit most any situation we choose to interpret in this way. Accordingly, there is no prescription for how to go about solving our problems; rather, it becomes a way of justifying whatever we happen to do, which, left up to our own devices, is nothing that we would not have done anyhow.

A more serious aspect of "fatalistic therapy" is the new order of fundamentalist religion sweeping many cities. Jews for Jesus, the Moonies, and other religious sects often attempt to get us to renounce "this-worldly" concerns and spend our full energies working for "the Lord". With Jesus to guide and protect us there is nothing we need worry about. Everything is preordained. If we don't find success in this world, then we will surely find it in the next, providing we live according to certain principles and work for certain religious causes.

While many of these religions claim to be addressing social problems — drug addiction, alcoholism — the manner in which they do so — through prayer, sacrifice, and repentance — does little to change the corporate structure upon which our society operates. We can certainly not pray away poverty or smog. But these new religions are not primarily concerned about these issues. The majority of their energies are put into recruiting new members and spreading the word. Presumably, if the word is spread far enough, problems will go away by themselves, since everyone will be leading a religious existence. Yet, since many of these religious cults require total devotion, the choice between watching a Colts' football game, drinking a can of beer, and maybe getting it on later with one's "old lady", *and* full religious devotion, often requiring strict celibacy, is not a very difficult one for most people to make.

Religion may enable some to cope, but for others, the sacrifice is just too great. Nor are many of us willing to relinquish our individuality, our manhood, or our natural look cosmetics for a life of religious salesmanship. And for those who do sign up, the ideals held out by previous converts often disappear as loyalty to religious dogma and service to the new high priests take precedence over building the new humanity and solving the world's problems.

There are some forms of therapy which claim to confront societal issues. Community mental health programs exist in many cities to help people living on poverty budgets address difficulties they may be having. Unable to afford regular therapy at fifty dollars an hour, community mental health workers often charge little for the services they provide. A person who is depressed because he is unable to find a job thus comes to the community mental health center for counseling and therapeutic assistance. Yet what does his "worker" tell him? How can psychologically oriented counseling, the background of most community psychologists, enable us to see our depression as a consequence of corporate profits and public priorities and that we are not to blame for the situation we find ourselves in. Understanding who we are, in this case, means seeing ourselves as victims of a society which does not have room for us. Accordingly, only a master magician could turn the tables on our depression, making us see that while employment is our problem, we are still in control of our destiny, master of our own fate.

Barring this charade, most psychologists can do nothing about the root causes of our employment problem, because they are not trained in community organizing or in social action geared toward creating more jobs. What happens in practice is that community psychologists, unable to solve their client's problem, simply listen to his troubles, or give him a battery of tests designed to find out what's wrong. Or, even more likely, they join the ranks of their social work brethren, moving cases in and out as rapidly as possible, keeping their clients off the street and out of trouble, rather than helping them organize to deal with the problems which led them to seek help in the first place. Community psychology, despite its lofty goals, then, often becomes a mental health maintenance clinic, where you go for patchwork, something to hold you over till your luck improves or they invent a new drug to cure poverty.

Community psychologists are not alone in their inability to see the social connections between our depressions, anxiety, neuroses and psychoses, *and* the social condition out of which these arose. Rather, psychologists in general are trained to study the individual in isolation from his peers. They have as little knowledge of how to change discomforting societal situations as we do, so why should we expect them to be able to do otherwise? As we pointed out in the last chapter, even marriage counselors, who at least deal with the individual in a group context — among family members — typically end up defining the "family" as the "isolated individual".

A girl comes home from school and refuses to obey her parents. After a few such rebellious episodes, the family calls a counselor and relates that they are unable to control their teenager. The family meets together with the counselor, who defines the problem as one of family communication. Nowhere does the counselor attempt to relate a perhaps boring high school curriculum about which the girl is powerless to do anything to the rebellion problems in the home. If he did, then he would have to figure out how the girl, with the support of her family, could attempt to change the school curriculum, a problem far more complicated in its scope than getting family members to "understand" one another. Nor does the counselor see that the basis of the girl's rebellion might lie in her recognition that the power her parents would wield over her is a compensation for the powerlessness they feel in *their* jobs, supermarket, and neighborhood.

V

Many of us need to get in touch with our feelings, have trouble communicating what is bothering us, and do not know how to relate honestly to other people. Some self-help oriented psychologists can give us insight into how we might better express ourselves. Still others of us are so severely depressed that we cannot relate at all. We too will need the help of a good psychologist in order to bring us back to reality. Yet, once the symptoms of our depression have been dealt with, we must begin to look at the underlying social problems which might have made us feel depressed in the first place. This is where self-help counseling, as currently practiced, leaves off, and a social understanding of our society must begin. Even if self-help therapy has been worthwhile, has let us express some of our feelings, there is no automatic transition between such expression and solving problems which plague us, despite what many humanistically oriented therapists might think.

Feeling good about ourselves rarely translates into

feeling good about our society. How could it, given the values which psychological therapy reinforces, and the manner in which such therapy is practiced? Self-help therapists want us to be honest with ourselves and with others, yet, how is it possible to be honest with ourselves when we have little understanding of our relationship to American society? How is it possible to be honest with others — such as our boss — when it might cost us our job? How is it possible to be honest with politicians when they do not represent us? In short, how is it possible to be honest and trusting in a dishonest and untrustworthy society?

Cures That Don't Work: Things Your Doctor Never Told You

10

As we have seen, many of the coping mechanisms we have described do not work. When our ability to cope in "normal" ways breaks down, we often become ill, sometimes fatally so. A salesman who cannot keep up the pace of having to find ever-increasing numbers of customers for his firm's products may at first seek relief in recreational activities, or immersion in countless hours of television viewing. Yet the pressures of his job remain. Finally, he suffers a heart attack and dies on his way to the hospital.

Others of us may respond to excessive stress and pressure in ways which are not as medically serious, but for which we still require the counsel of a doctor. Constant anxiety and frustration in powerless positions in school or work may lead us to overeat, taking refuge in another piece of pie, just one more cookie, steak, sour cream and potatoes. It may also lead to frequent headaches which aspirin cannot seem to relieve.

Nor may Rolaid provide comfort from recurring stomach problems, cramps, nausea, and diarrhea. Many of us too may suffer from an unidentifiable pain, a restless tension, sleeplessness, a feeling of empty sadness. Where can we go for a cure? Kaiser Hospital, in a recent study, showed that up to 60 percent of their patients sought the help of a doctor for emotionally related ailments. So what if we don't have any physiological symptoms; at least they will listen to us, at least they will prescribe a drug which will take away the pain of "living".

I

There are many reasons we seek the help of medical professionals for what are essentially personal and social problems. The most obvious one is that they can eliminate the symptoms of our stress. While they may have little to say on the social causes of heart attacks, if we arrive at the hospital in time, they *can* save our life. We put our faith in the doctor's ability because we have come to expect him to have an answer for what is the matter with us. Sitting there in her office, dressed only in socks and underwear, while she listens to our heartbeat with her stethoscope, makes us say "ah" with her tongue depressor, feels around our stomach to see if there are unusually tender spots, we feel we are in good "hands". She tells us we will have to undergo further tests before she can diagnose what is the matter, and we feel secure in her competence, though we begin to wonder what is wrong with our insides.

We follow the doctor's orders, drink a glass of berium, have x-rays done, and again return to see her. We have an ulcer, she calmly tells us, advising a diet we can follow, and pills we can take which will make us feel better. No matter what symptoms we describe to our doctor, we know that he or she will give us some sort of medical diagnosis which will enable us to understand what the cause of the problem is. This helps quantify the issue for us, put a label on it, and categorize it among other similar problems. After all, it's better to know what you have, no matter how serious, than to live under the constant anxiety of not knowing. The doctor eliminates any degree of uncertainty.

Not only do we find out exactly what is wrong with us, but responsibility for our symptoms is taken out of our hands. The sick role itself is a coping mechanism because it means that we are excused; excused from school, from work, from marital problems and hassles. If we are sick, then there is nothing we can do except place ourselves under care of a good physician who will help us get well at the same time as he is certifying the legitimacy of our problem.

While stress and anxiety in themselves might not be legitimate reasons for absence from role obligations, if we can develop symptoms that do fit the proper categories, our efforts will receive greater success. We are aided in this by the doctor's self-conception. Most doctors are unwilling to admit ignorance, to confess they do not know what is wrong with us. Consequently, they attempt to "round off" our symptoms into easily identifiable and known diseases. Or they shoot from the hip, operate now, and worry about whether they found anything later. Yet, since many illnesses have *social* causes, the effect of gaining medical attention will only make us feel temporarily better. In the long run, however, since the root causes of the problem have not been dealt with, the symptoms re-occur, break through the bandage, or pop out again in a new place.

Medical solutions are also popular because they are quick and easy. It's almost like buying a new dress. Simply open up your purse and pull out your group health care plan card, and get whatever services you need. Since you are not paying for it (though your company or the company your husband works for generally passes the premium on to you in the form of direct salary deductions or lower wages), there is no reason why you shouldn't take advantage of what's available.

For many of the poor who qualify for MedicAid, medical problems become a way of drawing attention to their plight and having someone listen to and hopefully help them with other difficulties they might be having. (We will discuss this in greater detail in Chapter 12.) Nor does it take much time to find out what's the matter and to start working on a cure. Indeed, the cures themselves are often quick and efficient. Take X number of pills for ten days, remove a gallstone, go on a sugar-free diet. Why mess around with lengthy analysis, deal with abstract "philosophical" questions about what may be other contributory causes of our problem?

Medicine often represents a technological solution to a non-technological problem. As we pointed out earlier, Americans have always had a propensity for such solutions

— the purchase of a new car to deal with the problem of low self-esteem; the development of a bigger and more deadly bomb to solve the problem of national security and ethnocentrism; the invention of space travel to take our minds off of dilapidated cities and occupational alienation. Medical research has taken technology to new levels. Expensive and elaborate medical machinery of one type or another lines many hospital surgery rooms. And like the feeling we get from eyeing the new gadgets prominently displayed in department store showcases, such medical technology indicates to us that doctors are really getting somewhere, they must really know what they're talking about, this must be progress. At the same time, the use of such equipment tells us that doctors are truly important people, because who else would be able to understand how this equipment works?

Despite this elaborate technology, however, doctors can often do no more than treat the symptoms they are presented with, for the social derivation of their patient's problems is seen as lying outside their jurisdiction. Or, more frequently, the issue of cause is limited to physiological questions doctors are most familiar with. A stroke occurred because of clotting in the blood. The liver failed to function because of too much alcohol in the lymphatic system. Diabetes resulted because of excessive sugar ingestion.

Doctors receive our trust because of the jargon they use, as well. Greeting us in white coats, having us sit before them unclothed, and having little knowledge of how our bodily system works, we are immediately powerless in their presence. How should we address them? Call them by their first name? Hardly. Then they begin to speak to us, asking questions. They understand. They know the names of all of our veins, our nerve endings, our bodily parts, and how they connect to one another. And they are names we have never heard of, let alone pronounce. Trachea. Esophagus. Tibia.

How might we talk back to these terms, or question the doctor's opinion? Then they write out a prescription for what ails us. More terms, this time chemistry words, rapidly scribbled on a white pad. 1300 cc of something. We obediently take it to the pharmacist, who hands us a bottle of tablets to take four times a day. Nor is there anyone else we can legitimately seek out for another opinion. Doctors have a monopoly on our health problems. They have spent countless years in post-graduate schools studying how the body works, learning their specialization and the terminology that accompanies it. Who are we, lowly patients, to call their expertise into question? And, of course, we do not want to; we want them to help us.

II

Many times doctors cannot fundamentally cure what bothers us, because they use a medical model to treat what are primarily social problems. The medical model specifies that all illnesses are caused by germs or viruses or some type of bodily disfunction, and therefore, all cures must focus on eliminating these bacterial agents, or finding a way of making the body function better.

Research money serves to legitimate this claim, as millions of dollars are poured into the American Cancer Society, the Heart Association and other organizations in the search for solutions. The medical model views the individual as the problem; therefore, it is only by treating the individual that the problem can be solved. How similar this is to other ways of coping. Since medical problems are personal problems, we are to blame for our illness, though doctors will assume responsibility for making us well. We can still maintain our *individuality* through the type of diagnoses we undergo (the problem lies within us); our sense of *control* in calling the doctor and following his orders; our *self-reliance* in watching ourselves get well. Never mind that these values have little to do with our new-found dependence on the medical profession, or our lack of power to change bureaucratic structures which might have caused our problem to develop in the first place. Yet, many of us are all too willing to relinquish our individuality in seeking medical advice, to see ourselves as another "flu case" or as suffering from "what's going around" or "what everyone has", feeling secure that we are little different from others, and that we can ride it out with little effort of our own. In either case, since we accept the medical definition of our illness, we are kept powerless to address underlying social conditions. Not only do we not see these conditions as part of the cure, but since the disease lies within us, there is nothing we need do except fix ourselves.

A good example of this kind of medical treatment can be found in the former best-selling medical book, **Type A Behavior and Your Heart.** The authors of this essay, drawing on their extensive research as heart surgeons, divide all people into two categories. Type A persons are those who are always anxious, worried, and nervous, and are typically, though not always, found in occupations which generate these kinds of psychological conditions. Type B people, on the other hand, are relaxed, mellow kinds of individuals, who don't let pressure get to them, and who are usually found in more easy-going occupations. After studying the literature on the causes of heart attacks, the authors conclude that Type A people are more likely to suffer this ailment because of the stress generated in their lives, especially when this stress is combined with a high cholesterol diet, or excessive calories, or excessive exercise, such as handball or jogging.

Since stress is isolated as a causal agent, the treatment regimen the doctors recommend for Type A people faced with potential heart attack is to avoid stressful situations, in combination with proper dieting and exercise. To avoid such stress, we are urged to slow down on our jobs, or seek out occupations which make fewer demands on our time and energy. This is especially true for those of us who have already suffered an attack. But what if stress is built into our economic system, is a part of organizational success? Why aren't Type A people urged to work on changing the values of the corporations which employ them, rather than leaving these corporate structures alone so that other Type A people who cannot resign or change jobs will suffer potential heart disease? The reason, of course, is because heart disease is viewed as a personal problem, Type A, and only personal solutions will suffice. A second reason is that major changes in the social order can be dangerous and stress-provoking; it is a lot safer and less stressful not to think about having to bring such changes about. Again, we do not define the social condition as the problem, nor are we prepared to bring about a social solution.

Some medical professionals do deal with preventive care. The medical sociologist and public health nurse attempt to educate people about living in a healthy environment. Rats should be removed from all dwellings, garbage frequently taken to the dump, and the house or apartment kept free of dirt. Children should receive immunization shots against polio, diphtheria, and smallpox. They should also be educated as to the dangers of smoking, venereal disease, and drug addiction. Upon release from a hospital, special diets are prescribed and advice given as to allowable work regimens.

Preventive health personnel do not urge us to take real preventive measures, nor do they engage in these themselves. Public health nurses do not lead attacks on the corporate profit system, or on coping mechanisms which leave us powerless, frustrated and insecure. Have you ever seen a group of medical sociologists chastise a large corporation for the excessive pressure it places on its workers? When have public health nurses recommended the closure of a department store because the purchase of superfluous commodities might lead to unhealthy relationships? Nor have we seen the development of legislation in this direction.

Part of the reason for this "failure" lies in the type of training medical professionals receive. Medical schools have only recently begun considering the patient as a whole person, rather than an assemblage of bodily parts. The great majority of a student's time is spent memorizing the names of nerve endings, studying how the body works, and performing rudimentary surgery. No time is left over to consider the societal conditions which may spawn disease.

Public health training focuses on how to prevent the spread of disease. Those sociologists who are employed on teaching faculties deal with such issues as the doctor-patient relationship and how to handle problems of grief and bereavement, worthwhile health considerations in themselves, but unrelated to dealing with the issue at hand.

Given the growth of group health plans in which potential patients pay a fixed amount per month and in return receive any services they need, it would seem that preventive medicine of the type described above might be much in demand because the more frequently an individual uses his medical plan, the less money a hospital earns. It would follow, then, that preventive medicine which kept individuals healthy might reap doctors and hospitals greater profits, as well as saving doctors valuable time, and helping them fulfill their medical oath of keeping as many people healthy as possible.

Yet, to the doctor raised on the tenet that the greater the number of patients and the more times you can see them, the greater the amount of money you will make, the practice of real preventive medicine becomes heresy. If patients became actively involved in dealing with the social conditions that bother them, many of the problems they now seek psychological and medical help for would soon go away. The only question that might be raised would be: could we stand a society without headaches? What would people have to talk about?

While much of the medical field focuses on the treatment of symptoms produced by a high pressure society — heart attacks, headaches, stomach disorders, the need to have someone to listen to, someone you respect, who understands — there is a far more sinister side to the problem. How can a doctor practice *good* preventive medicine and at the same time effectively treat someone suffering from the effects of a cancer caused by exposure to industrial poisons, asbestos fibers, or lead? And, how does the cancer patient cope with such exposure?

Told all medical problems are personal problems, the patient submits himself to hospital care, only once treated he may be turned loose in the very industrial plants which caused his ailment to occur in the first place. How many of these plants continue in operation despite the evidence linking their production to cancer? But the issue goes deeper, for, as we noted in Chapter 3, production is related to profits. Safety engineering costs money.

Smog, too, has been linked to certain types of cancer, yet the major auto manufacturing firms find it impossible to meet government pollution standards by the specified date. If automobile production stops because cars are unhealthy, then people will be thrown out of work. Unemployed, how will they be able to afford the consumer purchases which have become the mainstay of many coping lifestyles? Without the sale of asbestos for insulating our homes, where will asbestos workers be employed? Since the heart of our economic system, and of our society, revolves around the profit system, how is it possible to cure cancer without addressing the values which make pollution possible, profitable, and tolerable for those who do not currently suffer from it? Unable to confront the corporations that destroy them, the only way many industrial workers can cope with industrial disease is by seeing a doctor, but by then it is usually too late.

III

One of the reasons illness has become an acceptable way of coping for many of us is because of the temporary identity it supplies. We are sick, therefore we don't have to do anything. Other people will treat us with sympathy, often consenting to help us out in ways they would never consent to were we healthy. The housewife who has the flu suddenly finds her husband fixing dinner, doing the dishes, and putting the kids to bed. The grandmother who comes down with a bad cold receives phone calls and flowers from her younger relations, though they might never have taken the trouble otherwise.

The more rewarded for our coping, the less inclined we are to give it up. Being sick also enables us to indulge in our other coping mechanisms to our heart's content. The television can play all day; we can eat as much as we want; and get all the rest we can. Doctor's orders. Yet, we must be careful not to overstay our illness. The importance of this coping mechanism is that it be used only sparingly; otherwise, our employer, relatives and friends might cease paying us special attention, or paying us at all.

For some in American society, however, sickness has become a permanent coping mechanism. Older Americans, forced into retirement and living on social security payments plus a meager pension suddenly find themselves outcasts in a society which once valued their labor and appreciated their purchases. Cut off from job status and financial security, senior citizens find that they can no longer afford the "standard package" of weekly consumer purchases, expensive vacations, and new cars. Nor are they valued for the experiences they have been through, the knowledge accumulated from crises overcome, from having lived through several wars, and a major Depression.

Since our society primarily prizes technological knowledge, the older one gets, often the further away from "new ideas" one becomes, especially if we have held the same job for thirty years. Retirement simply puts us out of reach of such technological expertise, since it is reasoned if we did possess valuable knowledge, then we would still be employed. Nor does the wrinkled skin which aging brings match the youthful beauty held out as an ideal to emulate by television commercials and movie starlets. The end result of these changes is to force seniors into seeing themselves as parasites; no longer able to pretend to be the self-reliant individualists who were masters of the suburbs, supermarkets, and assembly lines.

Cut off from the mainstream, unable to lay claim to the prevailing value framework, and many of the coping mechanisms which have kept this value framework alive (superfluous consumption), many seniors take up permanent residency before their television sets, or, if possible, find comfort in bingo games hosted in local senior centers. Here, coping through television viewing and remembrance of things past become full-time preoccupations, as do checker games and poker. Told they are no longer participating members of American society, that their opinions and services are no longer needed, seniors attempt to make-do, often seeing *how long* they can stay alive, rather than focusing on the quality of their existence. Indeed, the questions of *how long* one has lasted, or been married, are often used as a means of trying to regain lost status, as if the quantification of survival could replace the emptiness now felt within that time span. Look, he's eighty-five and can still ride a bicycle; she's a hundred and one and can still talk.

Unwanted by their offspring, many seniors are shunted into old age homes, or develop illnesses which make full-time care a necessity. No longer able to find status and reward in a normal coping lifestyle because that lifestyle can no longer be practiced, they must face head-on their powerlessness to change the unacceptable position they now find themselves in. How can they do so? Who has prepared them? Sickness represents the only coping option left.

Old age thus comes to signify the crowning accomplishment of a society which rewards coping and does not educate its citizens on problem confrontation and resolution. Unable to feel useful, or even to pretend usefulness, we begin to find ourselves getting ill, our bones begin to ache, our eyesight begins to fail us, we can no longer get around like we once could. Told our bodies are not good for anything any more (not even sex), we follow the prophecy and begin to discard them. Our illness initially brings support from the social order. Doctors see us and listen to our complaints, providing we keep them focused on medical questions. Our relatives come from near and far to see what is the matter. Yet, as our illness drags on, they soon forget us again, it is no longer an emergency. We take refuge in talking with our peers who also suffer the same illnesses. We exchange stories about this pain or that; a kind doctor and one not so blessed. We form our own culture around illness, our own way of coping. Soon, our condition deteriorating and no longer able to take care of ourselves, some of us enter convalescent hospitals, where we await death or a chance phone call from a forgotten loved one.

And then we die. Isolated from relatives and friends who care, from neighborhood surroundings we are familiar with, the average stay in a "long-term facility" is thirty days. At the funeral, our relatives and old friends come to pay their last respects. Our children weep out of guilt and remorse, purchase an expensive casket to make up for what they have not done for us, the time they did not

159

have when we were alive to spend in our company, the energy they might have used to make our lives more meaningful, to give us an ongoing stake in American society, a piece of the action. They cope in the way they have always coped, and just as we did, by buying us things we cannot use, which are not bio-degradeable, and cannot filter down to meet us in the soil below.

Excedrin Headache 742: Spacing Out With Drugs and Alcohol

11

The freeway is crowded as usual as we drive home from work. Cars are lined up bumper to bumper, traffic starting then stopping, then starting up again. We reach into the glove compartment, open a small leather case, and pull out a number which we proceed to light up, inhaling the pleasant fumes, then slowly exhaling. Once, twice, three times we repeat this process. We turn on the radio; the sound is clear and distinct. So what if it takes us forty-five minutes to get home, we have become part of a procession, a parade of brightly colored cars. We become engrossed in the rock beat emanating from the radio speaker while our hands steer the car, the fingers gripping the wheel, the car going forward, because our foot has pushed the pedal, making the car accelerate and decelerate, focusing now on the foot within the shoe, and then back to the radio again, a whole world right here inside the car. Fascinating.

We look around at everyone else. They're so serious. What's there to be so serious about? Look at the way they talk to themselves, how they curse the cars in front of them. They don't see what's really going on. They don't understand. They're not stoned.

Perhaps we are not on the freeway. Perhaps we have decided to stop in at Ernie's for a quick one after work, just until the traffic dies down. Some other women from the office are going over. As we enter we see them sitting at "our" table. Hey, what's going on, we casually ask as a cocktail waitress brings us the usual. Not much. It feels good sitting here, all of us together, and three drinks later it feels even better. Everyone's so funny. None of the office formality. Real people, you know. Hell, I didn't know Sally was having problems with her husband, and that Sam was having trouble making his mortgage payment.

Getting stoned and frequent drinking have become significant ways of coping for a large number of people. Not only is it seemingly easier to face rush hour traffic and socialize with other people after a couple of hits, or a few drinks, but it's also easier to go to a boring class, do housework, or even make time go by. Other coping mechanisms we employ are also enhanced by our "high". Football games seem much more interesting if we have had a couple of beers, and sex is certainly far more enjoyable if we are stoned; we hardly have to worry about the procedures our sex manual told us to use for maximum satisfaction. Yet, while grass and alcohol are popular ways of coping, they represent only part of the arsenal of chemical additives we can ingest to escape problems we may have in our daily lives. If we are anxious, a visit to our doctor or psychotherapist can yield a prescription for Valium or Librium, which will relax us and make us forget about our worries; if we are having trouble sleeping at night, we can take Sominex or Nyquil; if we are having trouble getting started in the morning, we can take an amphetamine, or drink three or four cups of coffee; if we suffer from overdrinking, Alka Seltzer will relieve the pain; and headaches go away faster with aspirin or Bufferin. Add to this list the pills and liquids we ingest to get over the common cold, or stop our coughing, and the vitamins we take each morning to make up for a hurried meal, or a nutritionless diet of Big Macs, Ding Dongs, and cola, and we have an impressive list indeed.

I

Pills are taken for a variety of purposes and enable us to cope in different ways. Nor does the same drug work in the same fashion on all people. For example, for some of us alcohol is a real upper. We feel more sociable, outgoing and boisterous. For others, having a few drinks is a way of relaxing, depressing our emotions, helping us withdraw from a busy world. Marijuana tends to follow similar patterns. Many people just like to get high and listen to music and withdraw into their own "space", while others find it makes them more gregarious, able to participate more freely in conversations, and laugh at what might otherwise not appear very humorous. What we bring to any drug taking situation has an effect on how we will respond. If we tend to be insecure when we are "down", then, at times, this insecurity will be reflected in the kind of high we develop. Far from being a total escape, then, some drugs serve to reinforce the very problems we would retreat from. Most drugs, including alcohol, can be divided into two categories of coping behavior: other-worldly ways of escaping — Marijuana, LSD, and Mescaline — and drugs we use to support our position in this world — Valium, alcohol, and amphetamines.

Marijuana is a good example of how drugs enable us to escape our present situation. Studies of marijuana ingestion have shown that it tends to slow down our reflective abilities, thereby enabling us to consider the world in a nonreflective manner. What this means is that situations we took for granted are no longer stereotyped. When we are walking along a sidewalk, we suddenly become conscious of the sound of our shoes on the pavement, the cracks in the cement, or the color of the pavement. Not stoned, we would have taken the sidewalk for granted and thought about other, more important things. Stoned, there are no other things to think about, no priorities to set, no goals to meet; we are in the present and there is no place else to be. Objects come to be seen in themselves, without function. While we may be crossing a bridge, we focus on the bridge as a separate entity, rather than the function it serves as linking two points. Free from having to think about things in traditional patterns, and no longer tied to the past or the future, we can explore new ideas, or fantasies which play in our heads.

Our perceptions also change. The world we see can take

on any meaning we choose to give it. Skyscrapers can become large erections, trees turn into characters from novels we have recently read, clouds a battle between two opposing armies. As our reflective awareness or consciousness slows down, our sensory awareness is enhanced. Smell, taste, touch, are all perceptively clearer. We have time to feel the tiny ridges in our skin, to look into someone else's eyes, to taste ice cream and smell the flowers all around us. Freed from moral inhibitions, since the very concept of morality itself is tied to a certain conception of society, its place in history, and its value system, we can let ourselves go, and more freely engage in sexual and other kinds of activities.

Acid, or LSD, is a much stronger psychedelic than grass, and cannot be taken at full strength while driving down the freeway or working, though some people take smaller dosages and attempt to function in these roles. Acid tends to eliminate the reflective process entirely. Instead of thinking about the sidewalk we are walking on, we merge with the cement, there is no distinction between where we are and where it is. We have become the same entity.

As in more intensive forms of meditation, the self is lost, and we experience ourselves as part of the total universe. The chair on which we are sitting dissolves beneath us into molecules, we too have become molecules moving in fine patterns to the sounds of the universe. We are different colors, we are spilling across the floor, a rainbow without skin. Life is now truly meaningful, because the question of purpose and meaning has become nonsensical. We exist, we are, at one with the life force. When we die, we are simply changing forms, re-arranging our molecular structure. As such, there is no actual death, merely a reshaping of basic properties. We have not died, because *we* are not a separate entity.

Stoned on grass or acid, it becomes difficult to take our problems seriously, or, in many cases, to conceptualize them at all. Many people get stoned on their way to work or school, and stay that way for the remainder of the day, thereby creating a reality framework which never has to be questioned. This reality is reinforced by grass smoking or acid dropping compatriots who come to see the world in much the same way. A new subculture is created, replete with magazines (**High Times**), jargon, and status symbols. You haven't tried anything till you've had some Thai Stick. In the late sixties, when acid trips were more common, or more out of the ordinary, individuals were often ranked by the amount of acid they could ingest at one time (550 mics, 1000?), or by how many trips they had taken (50, 75). Today, acid causes little stir and getting loaded is a common phenomenon. The American Medical Association has even recommended de-criminalization of marijuana use. The acceptance of grass, however, has not meant that its function has changed. While no longer serving as an identifiable symbol of the counter culture, it does, among frequent users, still serve to set apart a distinct coping lifestyle, a way of interpreting the world and its problems.

If we are stoned, we no longer have to concern ourselves with conflicts in our life. Job alienation disappears, as work becomes interesting again. In fact, everything is now *interesting,* even the hum of the conveyor belt going by in front of us. Arguments about worker discontent are interesting, as are arguments against the fact that workers may be discontented. Or, none of it may matter. As our pain goes away, or is dissolved in laughter or innocent expressions, we become willing supporters of the status quo.

While our high may give us insights into the workings of corporate bureaucracies, it usually does not, nor does the process of getting stoned supply us with a rationale for how we are to go about changing those situations that alienate us. Equally important, when we are stoned we lose all motivation to become involved in such change because it no longer matters what kind of environment we are in. And, the stronger the drug, the more this feeling is accentuated. Gradually, we become spectators to whatever's on, no longer responsible for our actions, watching ourselves in the room, or simply watching others. How interesting. How funny. Without evaluation or moral judgment. Since we are no longer *in* the situation, it does not really affect us, and the politicans and executives who run our public and private corporations can continue to do so without fear of criticism or rebuke. Yet, when we come down, when our problems return, what can we do then, what can we say? Why say anything at all, why not simply go back up?

Psychedelics are popular because, contrary to consensual belief, they do not disrupt values promulgated by American society. They may liberate our sexual impulses and our fantasies, but they do not pose a major conflict with other values Americans hold dear. Like other coping mechanisms we would engage in, they represent a quick and easy solution to what might otherwise present an unsolveable dilemma. To a time-conscious populace, this is an important factor. So what if nothing happens while we are up or down, at least we avoided what was hassling us. In the same way, we are provided with a technological solution to a non-technological problem. The adage, *"science will save us"*, becomes a reliable ingredient in the philosophy of the individual dependent on his next "fix" for survival. After all, while *we* are coping, *others* may be coming up with solutions, new drugs we may take which will magically transform American society. Long time acid trippers used to say that LSD makes us experience the absurdity of our world, so that we will be free to create one more kind and gentle to our needs. Yet LSD did not bring about any new Mecca; on the contrary, it provided a chemical space in which to hide until it was safe to once again appear. The docility of chemical inebriation does not readily translate into the politics of social change.

Psychedelics also enhance our individualism. Able to retreat within the space between our ears, we are able to create whatever world we like, without having to risk putting this world into practice. Since there is no one to challenge our creation, we maintain ultimate control; we are all powerful. Yet our power is fictitious, a myth on which to build a kingdom unrelated to our real environment and the personal and social problems which inhabit that environment. Our energy and interest focused on the inside, we excuse ourselves from responsibility for what goes on "outside". That is no longer our society. Or, like our physically ill friends, we say we'd really like to get involved, but you see, we're stoned, smiling broadly to ourselves, want a hit? The drug removes any guilt we might feel and any sense of remorse for what we have not done. In fact, since we are not responsible, we are *free* to do whatever we want.

II

Psychedelics do, however, conflict with one major value in American society. They do not support the work ethic, especially if taken in excess. This is not to say that a large number of workers are not stoned while on the job, or that they're being stoned somehow sabotages the tasks they are trying to perform. Rather, psychedelics do not give us that get up and go feeling, they do not support the hard-driving executive or engineer who is trying to meet a deadline and needs a little extra push. On the other hand, alcohol, amphetamines, and even Valium do. While alcohol and Valium can be used to relax, often such relaxation takes place in the context of a job that must get done. Valium eases muscle tension and rattled nerves so that we can move ahead with the project at hand. It also makes it easier for professionals in positions of great responsibility — doctors — to perform their work without falling apart, enabling them to let go of the burden placed upon their shoulders. NoDoz and amphetamines keep truck drivers awake on twenty-four hour hauls.

Alcohol, uppers and downers are much more consistent with values promulgated by American society than are psychedelics. While psychedelics have us focus on an inner worldly or other worldly mysticism, uppers and downers enable us to accomplish pragmatic, down-to-earth goals. Indeed, many of these pills are the time-study man's delight, able to get maximum output from workers hyped up on whites. Here, have another one, it's on the company. The drive for business success, the little bit of extra effort put out to get ahead of the "masses" is, of course, consistent with the Protestant Work Ethic. It also matches our notions of individuality, self-reliance and control. The worker who can focus on a distinct goal and work as hard as he can to try and make it, is the Horatio Alger of our dreams. Amphetamines make us into super-beings, able to leap tall assembly lines with a single pill, work sixteen hour days, our pupils dilated, our heart pumping at three times its normal rate. And Valium gives us work without stress; an ideal combination.

But for how long? How long can the body continue to absorb these new ingredients — uppers for high performance at maximum speed, downers to ease our nerves in high pressure situations, and so we might sleep at night. While uppers and downers make us better workers, able to assume greater responsibility, they do not lead to changes in corporate policies which eliminate excessive stress and pressure and the continued use of amphetamines in order to keep our jobs.

Used to seeing us function at a particular speed, many corporations come to depend on that rate of output, drug-induced or not. Should we at some point refuse to continue such ingestion we might, at the same time, find ourselves among the ranks of the unemployed. Equally important, however, is that drug use of this sort reinforces corporate policies which generate the problem in the first place. While psychedelics make us into contented workers, happy to go along and accede to corporate demands providing we do not have to work too hard, uppers and downers serve to acknowledge and legitimate corporate and professional goals by reinforcing work ethic values. As a result, they enable us to cope with forces outside of our control. The power which the drug gives us, and which we then think we have in accomplishing great amounts of work, is really a powerlessness to change corporate priorities and policies, and a powerlessness to create our own value system and to escape the coping cycle. Nowhere do amphetamines show us how to accomplish this task; indeed, they detract our minds, our hearts and our energies from any such consideration.

Not only do uppers and downers help us achieve "success" within the work organizations which employ us, but they give us courage and inducement in other areas as well. Professional athletes regularly use pep pills which enable them to play harder, and provide greater stamina and strength on the football field. Cortisone shots are used to dull the pain of too many tackles, bruised ribs and thighs. Would such chemical support be necessary if spectators did not demand that their gladiators play to the "death" to win for them? Yet, with so much riding on each game — the vicarious adventures of millions of frustrated copers — how can a professional team not give their playing personnel the very best?

As we noted in Chapter 8, there is also tremendous pressure in our society on interpersonal relationships to satisfy all of our needs. The emphasis on successful hustling creates a good deal of nervousness in both men and women — in men worried about how they can approach someone at a bar or party; for women, in terms of whether they will be approached, and if they are not, what they will do. In order to give courage to our efforts, it is not uncommon to have a few drinks before addressing the lady of our favour. But, it doesn't stop here, because we not only want to make her acquaintance; we want to bed her as well. Myth has it that drink relaxes even the coldest heart (body), and such myths are readily reinforced by liquor company ads such as White Label and Cutty Sark, depicting women stretched out beside a bottle of their preference. Alcohol thus makes us into "real" men and women, at least temporarily.

III

Many of us switch back and forth between taking pills to pass exams or help us get that next promotion, and getting stoned to relax in the evening, listening to music, daydreaming off, making love. Nor, as we have noted, are drugs and alcohol necessarily used independent of other coping mechanisms. Neither uppers nor downers, grass nor acid can fundamentally solve the problems we face; rather, when used excessively, they serve to perpetuate these problems, turning us into drug addicts of one type or another.

The word "addiction" is crucial, for it symbolizes how many of us become hooked on coping, in this case drugs, in other cases, superfluous consumer products. We become hooked because we become overly dependent and build our lifestyle around the coping mechanism we have chosen. The less high we feel, the larger fix we need; the more frustrated we become at the failure of one dosage level of pills to relieve our problem, the more we crave a higher level, more consumer goods, more television, more gin and tonics, more lovers. Once addicted, withdrawal becomes more painful than consideration of alternative ways of dealing with our problems.

This is compounded by the fact that one coping device feeds off another, so that often to give up one is to give up all, a situation few of us are readily willing to consider. So we go on, our lifestyle nourished by our habit, dependent on it. Once in a while we think about our problems, but it's so easy not to. Once in a while someone screams at us on a busy street corner, waves a pamphlet or sign in our face, shocks us, but then we get stoned on the way home, turn on the tube, with a beer chaser. Maybe tomorrow. Later that evening, sitting in our living rooms, we feel smug and good as we watch a t.v. special on heroin addiction. Damn, we tell ourselves, how can they do it? What a waste. If I was like them, I'd shoot myself.

Cops, Robbers, and Welfare: Arresting the Symptom

12

Every two years we notice our television programming changing, at least temporarily. The family show we were used to seeing on Wednesday nights will not be aired because of a scheduled debate for two persons running for governor. Or, if it is a presidential election year, we might suddenly find ourselves watching a host of interviews with primary candidates. Actually it is little different than viewing professional football teams vying for a place in the playoffs. Just before the Super Bowl, we are able to witness coverage of the Democratic and Republican Party conventions, a true sports spectacular, replete with balloons, half-time bands, confetti, and speeches designed to please everyone.

We hear about the world we are so accustomed to avoiding, about the Middle East crisis, deteriorating cities, farm prices, the chances for a nuclear arms limitation treaty with the Russians, unemployment, and the lack of a balanced national budget. Depending upon whether we are hearing the incumbent or his challenger, we either find out that all of these crises have been adequately dealt with in the past four years, or that they have not, but will be if the challenger is elected. We also hear about the restoration of individual freedoms, trust and honesty, law and order, a new American dream.

After the convention, television viewing is filled with half hour specials, and commercial announcements by candidates packaging themselves, in the consumer tradition, for quick sale. If you vote for (buy) me, you will have an America you can truly be proud of, an America where no one need lack for a decent place in society, providing we all work hard and do our part. Finally, election day arrives. We take ourselves down to a polling booth in our neighborhood and cast our ballots for the candidate whose speeches and PR campaign impressed us the most. And we feel good, standing in line outside a friend's home, waiting our turn, feel good that we live in a democracy where we can choose our elected officials, who will watch over the land for us, making those "big" decisions so that we are free to focus on the "small" ones.

One man, one vote reaffirms our values, our individuality and independence, our choice of the kind of country we want to live in and how we want our problems solved. (It is, in fact, little different from the way we practice democracy in other areas of our lives, our choice [vote] of which channel on the television to watch, our decision about which brand to purchase, and the impact we have at the plant when our manager asks us what we think of the new air conditioning system.)

Then the election is over. We go back to what we were doing before and the politicans leave our t.v. screens and go back to what they were doing. Nothing very much changes, as we continue our coping lifestyle and they continue to run the country. While politics promises a way of resolving problems which confront us in our day to day lives, since politicans do not address our personal concerns, thereby leaving us to doubt whether in fact the things that bother us are legitimate grievances, we are little motivated to view the political arena as a solution.

Nor do most politicians take time to relate national concerns to personal difficulties. Beyond the gap between our view of the world and their views is the problem of how we might go about participating in politics even if we were so inclined. Having never been educated about polit- ical participation, beyond a memorization of the Bill of Rights and abstract high school civics class discussions of referendum and recall, we have no idea of how we might become involved in electing candidates who actually repre- sent *our* position. Besides, not used to participating in political campaigns, it becomes a lot of trouble to break the pattern now. It might entail changing a lifestyle we have grown used to and feel comfortable in.

And even if we did want to get involved, think of how much money that would take, what a half hour t.v. spot costs? And if they don't represent us, it doesn't really matter anyway, because we've got our lives to lead, and what they do in Washington has very little to do with what we do here at home. In fact, maybe next time, we might not even bother to vote . . . because this year they announced the winner on the radio before we even made it over to the polling place.

I

We may vote, or like vast numbers of our compatriots, we may choose to sit this one out; in either case, we guarantee that a sizeable percentage of our population will be unable to get jobs, will live in dilapidated housing units, at the core of rundown cities, often in poor health, attempting to eke out a living on food stamps and welfare payments, or on nothing at all.

How does this section of our population cope with being left out of the mainstream of American society — cut off from its jobs, its consumer goods, its feeling that "what's good for General Motors is what's good for the world"? How do they manage to practice values promulgated by our public education system, our t.v. networks, and corporate commercials, or cultures whose values are more consistent with the social conditions in which they find themselves?

The basic ingredient of living in poverty is survival. How am I going to get enough money to get enough to eat, to find a place to live, to treat the illnesses I develop, and in the process, how am I going to be able to feel good about who I am, and about the relationships I'm in. First, where do I get money? A typical welfare budget to a mother with two children yields around $450 per month, out of which she must pay about $65 for $130 worth of

177

food stamps. Food stamps only cover food, so she must spend an additional amount of money to acquire such things as soap, toothpaste, and aluminum foil. At this point, she is left with $385, providing she is able to feed her family on $130 worth of food stamps.

A two bedroom apartment will cost her at least $280 to $300, leaving $85 for clothing, transportation, baby-sitting, entertainment and non-food grocery items. If she has a car, one major breakdown will eliminate this mode of transportation, since she will be unable to have it repaired. She could, of course, get a job. Since most welfare mothers lack a college education, and many do not have a high school diploma, what jobs are available? She might decide to become a waitress, or work in an electronics plant, or in another position requiring unskilled labor. If she makes the minimum wage of $3.50 an hour, or even as much as $4, she will be able to take home less than $125 a week after deductions. Since she is working, her entire welfare stipend is taken away, nor does she continue to qualify for food stamps. In addition, her job will force her to pay childcare, since she is no longer home to take care of her young offspring. The $500 a month paycheck she receives will, when she figures transportation to and from work, amount to less than the amount she was receiving from the government for not working. Nor can she enroll in college since, if her children are over the age of six, she is required to be eligible for a job at any time.

Coping with poverty means more than attempting to live on a welfare budget, however. It also means that you will have to figure out how you are going to be able to live with a man and still hold onto your stipend since, if a man is found to be sharing your dwelling, your food stamps and welfare budget can either be reduced or cut off. It is possible to get married, but then you must figure out how to survive on $8 to $10K a year, the sum total of two take-home salaries in the unskilled labor market. Single men have a difficult time surviving as well, since many poor paying jobs which are open to women are "closed' to men. Attempting to carry on a meaningful relationship is also complicated by the fact that a husband may work night shift, while his wife works days. When are they supposed to see each other? Living in crowded housing conditions, three or four children in a single bed-room, under the constant pressure of trying to make ends meet, how can they find time for each other, even if they are home during the same hours? For the husband who cannot find work and whose wife must support the entire family, the frustration and anxiety he feels often contri-bute to marital conflict and physical separation. For who else can he blame, where else can he channel his frustra-tions except against his wife and children?

Coping with poverty means that you will have to figure out a way of rationalizing your position so that your life becomes bearable and meaningful. While you may live in a poverty ghetto, the outside middle class world invades your space, on billboards, on the radio, through television programming and commercials, and in supermarkets and department stores located nearby. How does one square his own position, his own lack of money, with the values he hears all around him?

179

Many do not attempt to bridge the gap at all, but rather become resigned to their fate, living day to day, without hope that tomorrow will be any different or any better. Others, however, attempt to find their manhood, their individuality, pride and power, and the money and material lifestyle which lends credence to it by joining gangs and committing what mainstream America labels crimes: burglaries, homicides, pushing heroin. Women become prostitutes to support themselves, their families, and their men. There is nothing sophisticated about many street crimes; many are simply carried out on the basic principle that might makes right, and if you've got a gun, or several big dudes with you, then you should be able to get what you want. It doesn't matter whether you get badly beaten up or killed in the process, because with nothing to lose you're better off trying to at least get *something* while you can, or before someone else beats you to it. You become a man by being able to take care of yourself, or by showing off your successful attainment of material acquisitions, by driving a new Cadillac.

Yet the power derived from engaging in street crime is limited to the inner city, power among one's peers. Unable to confront the outside power structure, to gain access to "white" jobs and middle class neighborhoods, the poor and nonwhite minorities must take out their frustrations on themselves and in their own neighborhoods. Crime becomes a way of coping, for even though one may temporarily gain the consumer goods of the dominant middle class, nothing has really changed — there is still the inner city *and* the suburbs; one's status in the larger world has not been fundamentally altered.

Nor is engaging in crime a way of solving problems of poverty, unless one wishes to make criminal activity a lifetime occupation. Even here, since criminal actions are primarily directed at those who can least afford them, the lifestyle one chooses is to the detriment of others who find themselves in equally dire circumstances. It becomes a war of all against all. The poor end up competing against each other for crumbs, a kind of bastardization of the free enterprise system and American idealism. In the process, they divide their allegiances, grow to hate and distrust each other.

Instead of poverty being a social problem having its root causes in the American economic system, it comes to be seen as a personal problem, which only the poor person acting alone can solve. Cut off from ties with his poverty-stricken neighbors, he is forced to fend for himself, find a niche and grab hold of it, be an entrepreneur. But isolated and without skills, he remains powerless to alter his situation and position in the larger society. Nor is he able to band together with others to gain greater leverage. While gangs do form, these are to maintain territoriality against the encroachment of other gangs, protection organizations; their purpose is not to build greater influence in the suburbs, shopping centers and corporations of America. Nor are the tactics of violence such gangs employ suited for the development of a larger power base.

Most of the poor do not engage in street crime, though they often find themselves the victims of it and the police typically assume that they want to break the law.

It is in many ways a kind of self-fulfilling prophecy. We find ourselves in a situation of poverty with seemingly no way out. At the same time, brightly lit consumer goods — status symbols — are held out, adding to our frustration. We commit a crime in order to achieve what everyone else has, and the police arrest us, or we get in a fight in a bar, or we beat up our wife, and the police arrest us. We go to jail, but since no other way has been found for us to achieve the goals held out by the larger society as worthwhile, we must continue to commit crimes. At the same time, public service bureaucracy budgets increase. There is a call for more money to hire more police to solve the crime problem. Our activities provide jobs for middle class Americans as cops, social workers, prison wardens, and parole officers.

We also enable middle class Americans to feel good about themselves; we reinforce their superiority by breaking their laws, and by acting in ways they find immoral. We tell them their values must be important and worthwhile, for how else can we explain the discrepancy between their success and our failure? Or, from the middle class perspective, we must be doing something right, or else we would end up being poor. Often, it is coping rationales such as this that help keep members of the middle class apathetic and indifferent to the plight of those not so "fortunate".

While the police and others may expect poor people to commit crimes, they also expect the "decent" poor to act like "normal" (middle class) people act, to find jobs and pull themselves up by their bootstraps. Middle class social workers treat welfare clients as if being on welfare is the client's fault. They often assume that the poor are too lazy, disorganized, poorly motivated, or have too many children (sexually promiscuous) to get work.

This results in what Ryan has called "blaming the victim", an attitude not inconsistent with the way members of the middle class view their own problems. It also places social workers in an interesting position. Workers are hired to help the poor deal with the problems of poverty, yet since they view poverty as a personal disorder, rather than as a social issue, they typically limit their role to helping the poor help themselves, which is interpreted to mean handing out stipends and food stamps, checking on welfare abuses and filling out forms. Instead of helping clients organize collectively to gain more power in their communities, to change legislation which will guarantee more jobs and better housing, they in effect tell clients it's up to them to figure out a way of getting off welfare. How the client is to do this, of course, is left up to them, though many caseworkers attempt to motivate their recipients with such subtle cues as: *How can you live like this?* or *How can you allow this to happen to you?*

The result is additional frustration for the welfare recipient and the chronically unemployed, as they find themselves unable to meet the expectations of those who are trying to "help" them. Unable to practice middle class values of self-help and self-reliance, dependent on low paying work or welfare stipends, distrustful of neighbors and lacking formal education and marketable skills, they are left isolated and powerless, and without a suitable rationale to justify their position.

Lacking control over outside forces, many of the poor are able to draw support from their cultural heritage, from the church, and from large extended families, especially in Chicano neighborhoods. Yet these support mechanisms, these ways of coping, are simply that; rather than building us up to do battle once again, or pointing out new strategies, they become ways through which we can hide our resignation, our failure and lost spirit. Others of us, having no viable church, no family, or ashamed of our position, turn to drink and drugs, or seek to be again with our friends in prison.

Still others of us recover from our dejection and go to a loan company, borrowing as much as we can despite exhorbitant interest rates in order to get a temporary fix, a new color t.v., a night on the town; to redeem ourselves. But our redemption is a brief one, though it serves to legitimate our faith in the system that all is well and good with middle class values, that we too want what everyone else has, and why shouldn't we? So what if the t.v. will be repossessed? It is our way of coping.

The rest of the time we must cope by reducing our expectations, by acknowledging our dependence on the welfare bureaucracy, by lowering our self-esteem and by getting what we can here and there. After a while, our motivation gone, we begin to feel comfortable, used to where we are and who we are, and intimidated by our failures we give up hope that things will ever be any different.

Every so often the coping mechanisms the poor use

are not enough to keep them pacified. It may be a particularly hot summer, or they may hear of new jobs for minorities, but never see any advertised in their neighborhoods, or the police may unduly beat up a couple of gang members, or an innocent bystander, and suddenly the whole fabric will come apart. In the ensuing riot the poor will be able to get out their anger, feel a sense of power, release their pent-up hostilities. Such 'violence' will once again draw the attention of middle class America, of legislators looking for votes, and corporate executives looking for tax write-offs and profits. New programs will be designed to meet the needs of the poor. Promises will be made, and the poor will go back to their homes, past looted stores and burned out markets. A small company or two will venture into the ghetto, hiring ten or twenty of the thousands of eligible workers. Health inspection teams will visit homes and apartment buildings and make recommendations. New poor will be 'discovered' and put on welfare. Riot leaders may be given jobs in a new 'community action organization' whose purpose is to clean up the neighborhood. They may be interviewed by city commissions, led to believe that they are important. For $15,000 a year they will have been bought off and given places among the middle class. For a while, the poor will talk about the riot, about their adventure, about the time they made middle class America sit up and listen. But, nothing will have changed. Later, when a small group of youths hold up a liquor store to draw attention to their situation, they will be arrested, the symptom quelched before it can spread and infect the whole body. In prison they will be told that it is their immorality that led to their containment. Only if they re-form will they be released.

Meanwhile, Standard Oil is fined $5,000 for excessive campaign contributions designed to influence the Presidential race. Other coporations are warned to institute smog devices in the cars they manufacture within five years because one-quarter of the population residing in certain cities may be susceptible to smog-induced cancer. Executives regularly engage in extortion and price-fixing, all of which goes unnoticed because they were only trying to make their companies more profitable and themselves more successful; they were only trying to fulfill the American dream.

PART II

Where Do We Begin: Society on the Couch

13

Though coping has become the dominant lifestyle for millions of Americans, it has yet to be labeled a problem, nor do those who are its most active adherents consider themselves to be doing anything wrong. Quite to the contrary, they are living up to cherished American ideals, fulfilling the American dream of individual success and fulfillment. In fact, many of us who have unwittingly adapted a coping lifestyle will take exception to the generalizations put forth in the first part of this book. After all, we're not alcoholics, we don't watch six hours of television a day, we don't see vacations as a panacea to all of our problems, we're not looking to have an affair; we're not hooked on Valium. Yet, we need not use any particular coping mechanism in excess to have arrived at the place where coping becomes a solution to most of the problems that confront us in our day-to-day lives. We may only watch two hours of television, but that two hours, in combination with one or two drinks before dinner, a visit to a nearby shopping center, a Saturday football game, and an hour or two telling ourselves we are okay, is all that may be needed. Coping may be a problem for everyone else, but it is our problem as well as the few minutes spent here and there begin to add up, until we find that all of our time is engaged in different kinds of coping activities, which absorb our energy and prevent us from doing anything else. In the end, it is our attitude which gives us away, the manner in which we confront uncomfortable situations, our attempt to escape, rather than solve the problems which plague us.

I

Though we may not define coping *per se* as a problem, it definitely causes problems for us. It leads to constant frustration as we search out a way of permanently avoiding the issues which trouble us. Yet, since coping has not addressed the problems we would run from, it can never satisfactorily deliver the panacea we hope for. Coping behavior in itself, moreover, prevents us from ever confronting our problems because we no longer consider such confrontation important, certainly not as important as choosing the particular coping mechanism we want to use for the evening. Instead of looking at the conditions which cause alienating work, we begin to agonize over the problem of boring television shows—why isn't there anything on tonight? If there's nothing on, then what else can we do . . . but we did that last night. Our attention shifted from the problem which generated our need to cope, to which form of coping can best enable us to escape, we are lead far afield from any solution. The failure of one coping mechanism to satisfy us leads us to seek out other coping mechanisms, rather than face the problem which caused us to cope in the first place. Coping also has us identify our predicament as personal in nature; only *we* can deal with our problems, and only *we* can solve them, or more properly put, only *we* can choose the kind of coping device best suited for our own particular needs. These needs tend to be an attempt to live out cherished American values of individualism, self-reliance and competition, which we are unable to practice in our classrooms, jobs, or marriages, but which we somehow feel hold a solution for what grieves us. Our 'solution,' however, keeps us isololated and powerless because it leads us to assume that we do not need others to help us solve our problems, and further, that the locus of our problems lies in our own heads, rather than in the social fabric of American society. If the root causes of our troubles lie in the social order, however, then we are obviously powerless as isolated individuals to do anything about them. Yet, the values we have adapted prevent us from confronting our problems in any other manner.

The frustration our powerlessness breeds may in some cases mean that our coping behavior will at some point get out of hand. That we will do anything to feed our 'habit,' to satiate our addiction. In the end we may become drug abusers, alcoholics, criminals, find ourselves on mental hospital wards, or end up with heart attacks, all the while thinking that we can still do it, just give us one more chance, our coping behavior will yet solve our problems, though it never does.

Coping not only causes problems for us, but it

causes problems for others as well. Our political indifference and apathy means that the government will continue to spend money in much the same way it has been doing for a good many years. Priorities will be based on who has the best financed lobby, rather than what *social* needs must be addressed. Defense spending will remain high, since such spending is a coping device the government uses to avoid facing the problem of international cooperation and global economic planning. Defense spending, like other coping mechanisms, however, is potentially unlimited in cost, since bigger bombs do not lead to a more peaceful world. The amount of money the government must spend on poverty, alcoholism, crime, mental illness and pollution will also continue unchecked, since such monies are not being spent to solve these problems, but rather to contain them. For example, if crime is a symptom of our social order, crime prevention must focus on dealing with the causes of crime, rather than on beefing up our police departments and arresting more criminals. But we would rather arrest more criminals. While the amount of money we can potentially spend on poverty is unlimited, government priorities and available tax dollars place a definite limit on how much is being spent. Money used to build nuclear warheads cannot at the same time be used to finance urban renewal projects which benefit the 'underclass.' Ultimately, wasted tax dollars begin to affect us, for example, when we are told that there isn't enough money to fund a viable national health insurance program, or rid our cities of smog, or, on returning from a vacation we find our color television missing and wonder why someone would do a thing like that.

Political indifference and apathy also lead us to accept the kind of economy we now have and to enable it to be a profitable one. Indeed, the same coping cycle that leads to unlimited and wasted governmental spending in certain areas also leads to unlimited consumer purchases of drugs, superfluous goods, alcohol, expensive dinners, homes we cannot afford, and visits to psychiatrists. It matters very little that our purchases cannot bring the salvation we had hoped for, since we are committed to buying as a way of solving our problems. When one product fails to deliver what the t.v. ad for it promised, we simply look for a new product which promises a better return for our money. The corporations which profit from our misguided allegiance also give us alienating work, necessitating the very relief our paycheck seeks to purchase. Such corporations also drain the earth of raw materials, stripping the environment in order to meet our insatiable appetites. In the process, they help legitimate the need for a large defense budget so we can keep 'cheap' products and a steady supply of raw materials coming to our shores. And the more we want to buy, the more new products handsomely placed in department store windows, the greater the chances of pollution, since the important thing is the finished commodity, the new gadget, rather than then chemical mixture which went into its manufacture.

II

It's easy to lay out the problem, is it not, but it's quite

another thing to think of a way out, to try and stop coping. The issue is made even more complicated when we consider the interdependent nature of our coping behavior. If we are to follow the analysis laid out in the first twelve chapters of this book, for example, it would mean that we cannot stop coping unless we are also prepared to drastically alter our economic system, since the kinds of coping activities we engage in are directly tied to corporate profit-making. If we stop purchasing superfluous consumer goods, then who will sponsor the television shows we so ardently watch? If we stop our weekly trek to the department store, then what will happen to our jobs? If we begin to question the products the company which employs us manufactures, and begin to demand a say in how such production is to take place, then what is to stop us from gaining control of the company? In a similar manner, if we cease our involvement with one particular coping mechanism, what is to prevent us from placing greater reliance on others? Must we stop coping entirely to be effective? Will not direct confrontation of problems in one area of our lives, for example, those we face on our jobs, create so much pressure that we must at least cope some of the time, especially since we are not used to taking a stand, to putting ourselves on the line?

The first task in ridding ourselves of coping behavior is to understand what it is, why it takes place, and why it cannot fundamentally solve our problems. This we have attempted to do in the first part of this book. Next, we must begin unraveling our dependence on coping. Change in this area involves focusing on the very coping mechanisms we engage in as a way of getting us to become involved in doing something about our situation. If we are rabid t.v. watchers, then we must use this as a focal point for a transformation of our lifestyle. We must begin to ask ourselves why the television set holds so much fascination for our lives, why we would rather be watching television than doing anything else. Ultimately, we will come to see the relationship between television watching and the personal problems we are faced with, but are unable to solve. Once we have reached this point, we must begin to ask ourselves how it might be possible to solve our problems. Do these problems affect other people besides ourselves, and if so, how might we make contact with them? If we can get a group of us together who are all bothered by similar problems, do we stand a better chance of doing something about our situation, than if we try to do it alone? An understanding of why we are powerless to deal with some of our problems as isolated individuals will in turn lead us to the conclusion that many of our problems are not *personal* at all, but rather, are social problems directly related to how our society is organized, the kind of business concerns we have, the type of governmental bureaucracies we have created, and the kind of values and priorities both government and business have set as guide-rules for our lives. If our social order is the problem, then it means that the social order must to some degree be changed if we are to rid ourselves of our personal problems and the coping behavior our powerlessness to deal with these problems has necessitated. The only way to change the social order, to deal with social problems, is to work with other people, so that we have more say and more power to bring about the changes we feel are necessary.

Our coping behavior is a good place to begin the process of social change, because this is where most of us place our interest and energy. This is what our lifestyle is all about. Many political groups which have tried to organize people around specific social problems have failed because they have ignored the lifestyles most of us engage in, and have not related the problems they wish us to concern ourselves with to the personal problems which are the basis of our coping behavior. They stand on a street corner urging us to sign a petition banning nuclear weapons, while we hurriedly rush past on our lunch break, our arms laden with packages. They want us to attend a rally on campus protesting the torture of Argentinian prisoners, but we have just gotten stoned, and the sun is shining, and we have an exam coming up in a couple of hours, and we don't know what they're talking about anyhow. They want us to vote a socialist ticket, but we have no idea what socialism means and how it relates to the Raiders—Vikings game; what it has to do with *our* problems. Besides, isn't socialism another form of communism, and who wants to live in a system like that? The more liberal among us smile when we see these different groups, feeling good about our country, that we live in a democracy where people can say whatever they want, and where we don't have to do anything to support them. How good it feels to be tolerant of others' opinions, especially when we have the freedom not to listen to what they are saying.

Many of the more radical political groups make the mistake of attempting to apply lessons learned in one country—China—to what is going on in the United States. They would push a particular line regardless of the social situation they are attempting to organize. There is only one way of seeing the world, and if you do not see it the way we see it, then there must be something the matter with you, since our political strategy is based on sound principles. Some political groups also restrict themselves to working with only certain types of people—minorities, members of the working class—feeling that all the rest of us are too corrupted to be "saved." In the process they use a kind of rhetoric (language) which has not been used in common parlance—if ever—for many years, and which not even the select few they would organize understand. Workers become the proletariat, the United States is an imperialist war-monger, middle managers are lackeys of the capitalist class.

If we are to be motivated to become concerned about eliminating coping and solving our problems, then we must start with where *we* are, with the things *we* think about, and the language *we* use to describe these things. We must start with the symptoms of our distress and trace these symptoms backward to their root causes. Only in this way can we hope to maintain interest and enthusiasm for what we are attempting to do.

Having established the basis for our problems in the social order, and recognized the need to work with other people to solve these problems, we can now begin to figure out how to begin. Labeling the social order as the problem may at first cause many of us to retreat into our bottles of Valium or our liquor cabinets, for the social order is so large, how can the six of us manage to change it? But it is not the *entire* social order that is initially our problem; rather, we are only concerned about those aspects of the social order which directly affect us: the company for which we work, the schools our children attend, the marriage we are in, the freeway we drive each day, the smog we must breathe, the neighborhood we live in. The question we must ask is: what power do we have, working with other people, to deal with our problems? Who else might we need to assist us? What other groups which are presently organized might support our cause?

We cannot reasonably ask people to stop coping unless we can show them that confronting problems is more. rewarding, not only because it will eliminate the frustration and powerlessness we feel when we are coping, but also because solving our problems is basically more exciting, more stimulating, and more fun. For example, what could be more adventuresome than to go against the social fabric, to attempt to build a neighborhood worth living in? What could be more exciting than attempting to create our own rules to live by? As we venture out to solve problems in one area of our lives, there will be others along the way to support us, friends to share our difficulties, and laugh with us at the frustrations we encounter. Nor do we have to give up all of our coping behavior during the first hour. We can still watch television, drink, get stoned, watch a football game or two, rather, what is important is the fact that we have begun, that our attitude has changed, that we are on our way. By focusing on the tip of the social order that immediately affects us, we can find immediate victories, signs of hope and encouragement to keep pushing, to try more difficult tasks, to solve more complex problems. And, the more control we gain over our lives, the better we feel.

III

Many of us will need help getting started, for it is one thing to understand the causes of our problem, and quite another to be willing to take the first step. Since many of us are already seeking professional help as a way of coping, it would be possible for those of us seeing therapists, drug counselors, medical doctors and others to request that they aid us in solving our problems rather than helping us to avoid them. Suppose, for example, that instead of visiting our psychologically trained and oriented therapist who told us our problems lay within our heads, we were to visit a sociological therapist, who pointed out possible causes of our problems in the job we held, the schools we attended, and in the way in which our neighborhood was organized. Instead of trying to get us to "reason" our way out of our frustration, anxiety and anger, he or she would attempt to get us to focus our frustration and anger on the problems generating these emotions. They would also put us in contact with other people faced with similar problems, and work with us as a group to devise strategies for social change. Such a sociological therapist would need a background in community organizing, an ability to discuss the symptoms of our problem at the same time as they got us

197

to connect these symptoms to underlying causes in the social order. The sociological therapist would ask: what is there about our social situation or the way in which our community is organized that might have caused us to feel constant anxiety, sleeplessness, or inner turmoil? rather than, what is there about the way our personality is organized that might have caused us to feel these things. The difference is fundamental.

Sociological therapists might come to replace existing drug counselors, alcoholic advisors, psychiatrists, and marriage counselors or, those presently occupying these positions might make the transition themselves. How much better a drug counselor might feel if he didn't keep seeing the same faces over and over, how much less frustrating his job might become, and as a result, how much less *he* would need to cope. In fact, those of us presently involved in the helping professions might see a change in how we perform our jobs as a way of breaking our own coping lifestyle. Beyond the therapeutically-oriented helping professions, social workers, unemployment counselors, and eligibility workers can be called upon by their clients to change the manner in which their jobs are performed. Welfare recipients can demand that social and eligibility workers help them solve the problems of poverty, rather than blaming recipients for the poverty position they find themselves in. The effort here would entail far more than dispersing "survival" funds; rather, welfare and unemployment insurance recipients would be helped to understand the roots of their problem as lying in government priorities and corporate profit making. The poor and the unemployed could then be organized into groups to lobby for a change in government spending, for more jobs and better housing. These organizing efforts would transform the position of the poor from one of blaming themselves for their position, to blaming the government and large corporations. Instead of turning their anger and frustration inward onto themselves, leaving them defeated and unmotivated, they can begin to direct their energy toward institutions which promise a solution. Again, the focus is on the problem underlying our coping behavior, not on an abstract goal or target. And again, the issue is: what is there about the way society is organized, and the priorities it holds that causes forty million of us to be poor, and ten million of us to be unemployed?

Sociologically oriented practitioners might also become a part of the medical profession. Since many of us visit doctors because of emotionally related disorders, being able to see someone who enabled us to understand the social basis for our medical problems would go a long way towards contributing to our good health. Stomach disorders and headaches would come to be seen as symptoms which could be treated by addressing the causes of the anxiety creating them. More serious medical problems, such as heart attacks, once our physiological processes had been restored to normal, might be treated in a similar manner. Patients might be organized into action-oriented teams bent on eliminating overly stressful work situations, so that others as well as themselves might not suffer recurrent heart problems. Such sociological practitioners would free medical doctors to work on reducing the physiological symptoms their patients experience, as well as to focus on problems which were more biologically oriented—those generated by viruses and diseases. It would also reduce the doctor's caseload, since most of us would begin to seek other solutions to the problems we were faced with, and because many of our medical problems would have been solved. Sickness as a way of coping would no longer be needed. As we noted earlier in this book, hospital plans based on preventive health, that is, group payment plans, would also save money since fewer people would require hospital services. It might not even be necessary to hire sociological medical practitioners *per se*, rather, it might be possible to change medical school education, and to re-educate doctors as to the need for more social cures and how these might be brought about; to switch from a medical model which sees illness as a personal problem to one which asks what it is about the society in which we live that has caused us to become ill.

Labor union members could begin to ask their leaders to consider quality of work issues (what should be produced, how it should be produced), rather than continuing to focus on more bread and butter concerns (improving the fringe benefits, increasing our paycheck). Any such discussion within a union would begin to address problems of worker control and power over situations that directly affect them. A union member might bring up the problem of assembly line alienation and how the plant might be better organized. A discussion of different types of job rotation and decentralization might follow. How might the company be motivated to change its organizational format?

The union could point out that if workers were more involved in what they were doing, that is, were less bored, they would probably work harder and the company might reap greater profits. Moreover, effective union leadership could enable employees to see that it isn't their fault they are bored, but rather the blame might lie with the type of corporate leadership controlling the place in which they work. Production line reforms may not be enough; rather, workers might come to demand that they have a say in what the company is to manufacture, and in the design of the product itself. This in turn might entail a discussion of whether or not a certain item is worth producing, that is, does it satisfy a social need, or is it being produced because the company feels it will make a profit? Public service employees can begin asking similar questions of their leadership. A social worker, for example, might ask why her agency is not accomplishing what it is supposed to be accomplishing, why it is so embroiled in red tape and bureaucratic procedures that it is unable to effectively deal with problems of poverty. As workers begin to ask questions, or to get their unions to ask them, and to develop programs designed to get meaningful answers, they find less need of rationalizing their position, or daydreaming off, of seeking ways to cope both on and off the job.

Consumer advocates in every community might be funded and staffed by city, county, state, or federal governments, to help us see the difference between buying something because we really need it, and purchasing that item because it enables us to cope better. *Caveat Emptor* — let the buyer beware — would be carried far further than warnings about faulty manufacturing or construction of specific products, or potential dangers to health. Rather, the buyer would be urged to beware that they are buying, and how such purchases affect their ability to solve problems in their daily life.

This would be especially important in the case of drugs. The surgeon general's warning on cigarette packages might be placed on every bottle of Valium: **Warning: the contents of this package may render you unable to effectively deal with your problems**. Consumer advocates might have storefront offices in every shopping center and business district, where they would be available for consultation, for disbursement of literature and advice.

License challenges of radio and television stations on the grounds that such stations do not serve the public interest might lead to the creation of different types of newscasters, who tell the news of the day from the perspective of the lifestyle and problems most of us engage in. Such a newscaster would be able to relate national problems to local concerns; and to get us to see our personal problems from the perspective of social issues currently plaguing the larger community and society.

Newscasters would not only be able to show the interdependent nature of personal and social problems, but would also be able to demonstrate what various groups might do to solve these problems. Case studies of existing group actions might be highlighted, showing how a specific group of persons shifted from using coping as a way of avoiding their problems to the particular social action tactics they engaged in to transform their situation. Such a depiction need not be a whitewash, but rather, would point up problems this group encountered, and how these problems were overcome. Consumer complaints to t.v. stations might also force the creation of different kinds of television programming, with such shows as *Community Organizer, Neighborhood Activist, State Legislator.*

Specific one hour specials might also be created to deal, in a fictionalized way, with how we might stop coping and begin solving various problems we are confronted with. A critical look might be paid to the sports spectator, the real impact of vacations on our lives, or to how children sought to make their educational experience more meaningful.

New kinds of curriculums, teacher, and recreation directors might also be trained and developed in order to examine coping behavior in its initial stages and to teach students how to solve their problems so that coping might never be necessary. This topic will be explored at greater length in the next chapter.

Finally, police can change the manner in which they perform their work, and the attitude with which they view criminal problems. Instead of seeing crime as inherent in the moral character of those who break the law, they can begin to understand crime as a symptom of a society which cannot fulfill the needs of its members. What is there about the way our community is organized that caused our t.v. to be ripped off, that caused the corner liquor store to be broken into, that caused that guy to embezzle $400,000 from the bank he worked for? Is there some relationship between middle class juvenile delinquency and boring and irrelevant high school curriculums, and, if there is, how might the police help those committing these crimes to address the problems that caused them to cope in the first place?

In this kind of police perspective, the word *police* itself might be changed to *community facilitator*, signifying someone who helps us solve "street" problems. Such facilitators might work hand in hand with social workers, teachers, therapists and others to help us organize collectively to find solutions to our problems, thereby preventing criminal actions from ever having to take place.

IV

Where will these new professionals come from? Who will demand that these positions be created? We will. But new occupations are not enough, nor can we rely on these new professionals to "save us". By focusing on the tip of our problem, on the coping mechanisms we have chosen to use, they can help us redirect our energies and attention to the causes of our problems, and they can help us organize collectively with others to solve these problems, but it is only through *our* actions that anything will ever get done. The social order and the way in which our society is organized may be at the base of our troubles, may be causing us to feel isolated and powerless, to seek out coping mechanisms to make our lives bearable, *but* only if *we* gain power, if *we* act to change the social order where it impinges on our lives will our troubles be eliminated. The social order will not change itself.

It is also important to realize that many persons now in power, who hold high positions in government and industry, will be unwilling to grant us the solutions we seek to our problems. They have too much invested in terms of the profits they make and the status positions they hold, to willingly consider the alternatives we propose, for in some ways a gain in our power means a loss in theirs. They too, however, live under many of the same pressures that we do, pressures to maintain their position against all competition, pressures to seek greater power, to constantly stay ahead. In the long run, they too stand to gain from a change in the social order, a shift to the philosophical premise of we-all-win or we-all-lose, rather than the one of I-win, you-lose which they currently seek to maintain. This will be explored at greater length in the final chapter of this book.

In the short run, however, those in power will seek to hold on to their position, so it is incumbent on us to be able to understand the kind of leverage we can best use to alter their situation. Once organized into action groups, how might we best gain power? The strategies will vary depending on the particular situation we find ourselves in. Members of the middle class have power as consumers. By boycotting shopping centers, they can have a fundamental impact on the economy. Persons on welfare lack economic power, but they do possess potential political power in the votes they can deliver, and in the amount of "free time" they can spend campaigning for a candidate who promises to represent their position. To gain such power, however, we must be willing to use it.

Education for Problem Confrontation

14

Our public school system can have a lot to do with getting us out of a coping pattern and preventing one from ever getting started in the first place. Yet, in order for this goal to be achieved, we need a new type of educational curriculum and a different kind of teacher. The curriculum must be interdisciplinary in character, and it must focus on solving problems which confront students in their everyday lives, as well as on solving those issues plaguing the larger society.

I

At the elementary school level, such a student-centered, problem-oriented, interdisciplinary curriculum might be developed along the following lines. The individual student would be conceptualized to exist in a variety of social or spatial situations which might correspond to different areas of current educational specialization:

The Self in Space — Social Geography
The Self in Time — History, Current Events, the Future
The Self in Culture — Anthropology, Ethnic Studies
The Self in Society — Political Science, Economics
The Social Self — Sociology
The Self in Nature — Environmental Studies,
Biology, Botany, Physics, Chemistry, Geology
The Self in Technology — Engineering
The Self — Psychology

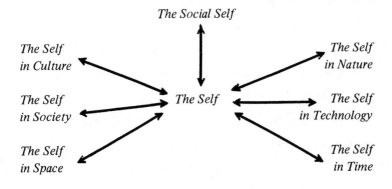

The individual student is not only seen in various social and spatial situations, but each aspect of the self is conceptualized from an individual perspective. For example, when a student is asked to think of historical events, he first thinks of how such an event affects him. If he is thinking of social geography he might first ask, "What are my immediate surroundings, what is my house, my apartment, my classroom like?"

Second, he might focus on any problems that exist in his spatial location. Is his house too noisy, too crowded? Is the neighborhood littered with trash and broken bottles?

Third, the individual student is asked to find possible alternatives or solutions to the problems he has enumerated. Perhaps a re-arrangement of family members' schedules is possible so that there are quiet times in the house or apartment. Maybe the family could install acoustical soundproofing in certain rooms.

Finally, the student is asked to develop and implement strategies for bringing these alternatives or solutions into existence. Different members of the class might take the roles of a particular classmate's family and "role play" how the problem of noise and overcrowding might be broached, what possible parental responses might be, and how these could be dealt with.

In short, in every social or spatial situation the student deals with four key questions:

What is the situation like?

What problems exist in the situation?

What alternatives or solutions are possible
for alleviating these problems?

How can these alternatives or solutions be brought about?

Utilizing the student-oriented social problems curriculum allows students to think and act upon those things which directly concern them. From this level of direct experience, students gradually work "outward", away from themselves to more abstract questions and problems. Regardless of how far removed from the individual's life the curriculum might get, it ultimately relates to the individual student's direct experience. Rather than trying to learn an abstract generality which at some point in the future applies to reality, the student is able to begin with that which is known, and *then* gradually derive the more abstract, general concepts. During the entire process, the need to become involved and *solve* problems is central.

Another aspect of the student-oriented, social problems curriculum is that subject areas merge and become interdisciplinary. Students quickly perceive that no single area of social studies is exclusive of any other area. For example, they realize that problems in the area of social geography cannot be solved without reference to economics, sociology, political science, and so forth. The higher the grade level, the more vivid the interrelatedness of subject area becomes. Nor is the interdisciplinary nature of the curriculum limited to fields encompassed under the social studies rubric; rather, reading, writing, and math become important ways to explore and convey a myriad of social studies concepts. Students learn the three R's as a means or method for gaining a better understanding of the problems encountered in their everyday world. No longer must they spend an hour writing about "nothing", or doing math problems which have no reference to problems they may be concerned with. Equally important, the sciences are not split from the social sciences. The student comes to see himself in a physical as well as a social world, one which presents challenges and problems he must deal with, and which begins to acquaint him with the moral decisions he will have to make concerning the development of different forms of energy, and new technological products. No longer will he be able to view science as a neutral subject having little impact on his life.

How does this student-centered curriculum actually work? Here are some curricular examples written from the perspective of someone who might teach in this kind of program.

FIRST GRADE: SOCIOLOGY *(The Social Self)*

Ask students what makes a friend. Have them draw a picture of a friend. Why do you like some people and not other people? What do you do when you don't like someone? What other things could you do so that the people you don't like become the people you like? Draw a picture of how you see yourself. Draw a picture of how you feel when you don't like someone. How do you feel when no one wants to play with you? What do you do? Do you think boys and girls are different? How? Can boys do things that girls can't do? Act out some of these things. Can girls do things that boys can't do? Act out some of these things. Why does the difference exist? Do you think you should be able to do whatever you want regardless of whether you're a boy or a girl?

SECOND GRADE: *(The Self in Space — example*
SOCIAL GEOGRAPHY *for a school with a walking population)*

After class members have drawn a floor plan or picture of their house or apartment, discussed problems they encounter in their living space and how such problems might be resolved, have them carry out the same series of questions with respect to their neighborhood. Since many students at this age have a difficult time understanding the concept of neighborhood, the class might go on a walking tour of the area surrounding the school. The students carry individual street maps. As the tour continues, each student can mark where their friends live, where the local market is situated, busy intersections, and so forth. After the students return to class, an enlarged map of the neighborhood might be placed on the chalkboard and the residences of class members located on this map. A discussion of environmental problems related to the neighborhood layout might follow. A busy street divides a section of the residential area from the school and there is no overpass. School grounds are closed after school and there are no nearby parks to play in. Back yards are separated by high fences; there are no play areas around apartments. Focusing in on one problem, the need for an overpass, class members individually or in groups write letters to the city planning, traffic safety, or public works commissions asking them to look into the matter. Visits to the commission offices or meetings might also be arranged.

THIRD GRADE: *(The Self*
POLITICAL SCIENCE *in Society)*

At the beginning of the semester pick three consecutive days when it would be possible for students to do whatever they wanted in the classroom for a period of fifteen minutes each day, provided they do not leave the room. This fifteen minute period should end with a scheduled recess. After the three days ask the class how they felt about the free period. What things did they do? Why? Do they think the class should be conducted that way all the time? Why? Why not? Are there any rules which might be necessary in the classroom? Draw up a classroom bill of rights. What happens if someone breaks the rules? Is everyone obligated to obey the rules? How can the rules be changed? Should anyone have a greater say in what the rules are or about what happens in the classroom? Should the teacher? Why? What if the teacher breaks one of the rules we have agreed on? Compare your classroom bill of rights to the rights you have at home. Do you know what these rights are? What rules do you have to obey at home? Why? What rights do your parents have? Your brothers and sisters? Are the rules in class different from the rules at home? Compare the bill of rights for the classroom and the bill of rights for your home. Read the first ten amendments of the United States Constitution. Why do you think these ten rights were made into laws to live by?

FOURTH GRADE: *(The Self*
ECONOMICS *in Society)*

Have students pick five advertisements they frequently see on television and write a brief explanation of *why* the advertisement wants them to buy that particular product. Do the products work the way the advertisements say they will work? How can you find out? Have your students pick an advertisement they think may not be telling the truth and write a brief paragraph explaining what they think the product really does for them, if anything. What values do the five ads each student picked emphasize? How do these values compare with their own values? What things do these advertisements tell us about what we consider important in American society? Why do we consider these things to be important? What would our lives be like without these products? Could we survive? Have each of your students make up two advertisements for things they consider important for people to know about or have (e.g., something that protects the environment or saves lives), and have them present these to the class. Ask the class how they could make people aware of some fact or product or idea without using advertising.

Take your class to the supermarket and have them make up a grocery list of all the food items they would need for one week's meals. Have each student add up the cost of their list. Ask them why some lists cost more than others. Give an explanation of unit pricing and how it is possible to calculate the prices of a single item packaged in different sizes. Conduct a discussion about why people have to pay for the food they have in their shopping carts, why they can't just walk out with what they need. Why do people have different types of food in their shopping carts — i.e., some people have t.v. dinners, others have steaks? Food often represents different cultural values; ask your students to consider what different types of food tell us about the culture which that food represents, e.g., tacos. Is there a relationship between geographical climate and cultural preference for a specific type of food? (pineapples — Hawaii — warm?)

FIFTH GRADE: *(The Self*
HISTORY *in Time)*

Have everyone in class make a list of events they consider important that happened in their lives or in some way affected them the previous month. Why were these events important in relationship to previous important events that had taken place over the years in their lives? Have students bring copies of magazines (**Time, Newsweek**) or newspapers which describe events taking place during the same time period (the previous month) to class. Also have students ask their parents what they considered as important events during the same period. Attempt to arrive at a consensus based on the newspaper, magazine, and parental accounts of what the press and parents considered as significant events. How do these compare with the events students listed? Are they more important? Why? Why not? Is there any relationship between the student list and the list from magazines and newspapers? How do events which happen in students' lives relate to events described in the newspapers and magazines? How do events get in the newspaper; who decides they are important? How could students get something in the newspaper they thought was important? Start a school/neighborhood paper which relates national and local newspaper stories to the daily lives of kids in the neighborhood.

SIXTH GRADE: *(The Self*
THE FUTURE *in Time)*

Have your class make a summary list of the problems

facing the school, neighborhood and society in which they live. Have them also make up a list of what tasks might need to be accomplished to enable our school, neighborhood, and society to survive. Have them then design an alternative school which solved these problems and discuss how these alternatives might be brought about. Each unit can in turn be broken down into smaller categories such as the curriculum of the school.

All of the "social studies" areas are taught at each grade level, and each year the four-question approach is repeated throughout the curriculum. Questions, exercises, and activities become gradually more abstract and difficult as the student's world and world view expand. The social geography of a sixth grader encompasses a far wider area and set of problems than those which confront a first grader. Within each grade level, one social studies area builds on all of the others. For example, the development of a classroom bill of rights and responsibilities (self in society: political science) naturally leads to a discussion of an economic and familial bill of rights which in turn raises questions about how people should relate to each other (the social self). Nor can such a discussion be divorced from where people live (social geography) and values different people have which they might wish to preserve and practice (the self in culture). At the same time, a classroom bill of rights can be put into historical perspective with readings and films dealing with other such documents and the social conditions which lead to their creation (the self in time).

Not only is it possible within such a curricular format to combine disciplines with methodologies (art, music, the three R's), but it is also possible to bridge the gap between our physiological self and our social self, or between physical education and mental education. Playground directors and teachers can urge students to make up their own games, perhaps games based on the concept of all-win or all-lose, rather than the kinds of I-win, you-lose situations most students are now encouraged to engage in. This doesn't mean that traditional sports activities should be eliminated, but rather the rules by which such activities are practiced should be re-examined, and if they are still considered necessary, re-created by those who will play them.

Using the student-oriented social problems curriculum, students, in conjunction with their teachers, create their own lesson plans. Such lesson plans of necessity emphasize group cooperation in solving problems, since students learn that their personal problems are often caused by the community and society in which they live. As they learn to work together to solve problems, they come to realize that they have some degree of power to change situations they do not like. They learn different ways of organizing collectively by putting such principles into practice. As they learn to work together collectively, they also learn that knowledge isn't something that one person has, and another doesn't, but rather, that everyone must come to have an understanding for any one of us to solve the problems we are faced with. Students thus come to teach one another, and the teacher, while acting as a lesson facilitator, directs and expands students' narrow concerns into the context of wider societal problems. The student-centered social problems-oriented curriculum provides an opportunity to bring relevance and meaning to our educational system *without* sacrificing educational quality. In the process, we will have taught students how to avoid being hooked on a coping lifestyle, by motivating them to deal with issues affecting their everyday lives.

How might this curriculum be initiated? At every elementary school there are a few teachers (with tenure) who are already trying parts of this curriculum in one form or another. They must be encouraged to test out the curriculum on an experimental basis, perhaps one class from each grade level. Interested parents can approach teachers, principals, and members of the school board, urging that this kind of curriculum be adopted. If the curriculum is adopted, parents should also be willing to work alongisde teachers, providing guest lectures on particular problems they have some experience with, or simply working the curriculum through with their children, since the issues their offspring will be concerned with will directly affect parental lives.

Parental support will also enable students to have greater power and leverage in solving their problems, as well as providing encouragement for students to become involved in particularly difficult issues. Teachers' unions might also push for the adoption of such a curriculum, focusing their attention on quality of education goals, rather than sticking strictly to bread and butter issues.

Once an experiment has been tried at one school in a district, it sets the stage for experimentation in other schools, or for mass adoption. If teachers can show that students will learn the basics better under a curriculum which relates to students' everyday lives, then such a curricular change will have overcome at least one hurdle on the road to formal acceptance and implementation.

Teachers can also learn how to develop a student-centered social problems oriented curriculum through in-service and pre-service training programs in nearby schools of education. Teacher training in this kind of curriculum would be expected to differ considerably from what now passes for teacher ed. A prospective teacher would have to have some experience in solving problems and in community organizing, so they could convey this experience to their pupils, not in urging their pupils to follow in their footsteps, but by providing an example of what kind of change is possible, and to be able to understand some of the difficulties and problems students will experience in trying to solve their own problems. Perhaps, at least initially, the best teachers of such a curriculum will come from outside formal educational institutions; people who are already practiced in problem confrontation and solution.

II

High school curricular changes cannot be divorced from changes at the elementary school level. Students passing through the elementary school curriculum described above will not settle for the kind of fragmented, irrelevant curriculum most high schools now offer. Yet even without such an elementary school background, high schools can be transformed in ways which will enable students to feel that they are playing a meaningful role in society, as well as enabling them to confront problems they may be faced with.

At the outset, a high school survival curriculum must be initiated. Such a curriculum might take the place of the senior year, or be spread out over a four year period. At least five courses would make up the topic of "survival": a course in fix-it technology which would enable students to understand and be able to repair their car, washing machine, television, radio, and other household appliances. A course in consumerism which would acquaint students with the concepts of built-in psychological and techno- logical obsolescence in the products they might buy. It would also help them evaluate whether they are purchasing something because it enables them to cope, or because they really need the object of their desire. A third course would cover basic health, and the relationship between ill- ness and society. Such a course would enable students to treat many of the ailments they experience, as well as being able to diagnose other illnesses as symptoms of personal and social problems they are unable to resolve. This course would also evaluate the use of drugs and alcohol as ways of coping. A fourth course would teach students how to organize collectively to deal with prob- lems they might currently face such as unemployment, lack of power to change school curriculums, and family problems, as well as problems they may run up against in the future. A fifth course would be entitled basic law, and would acquaint students with their rights — how to initiate changes in the law, and what to do if they are arrested for a criminal offense.

Beyond this basic survival curriculum, more fundamental changes might be put forward. As we noted in Chapter 2, most high school aged youth are forced to adapt a coping lifestyle because they are not considered valuable members of society with meaningful roles to play. To reverse this situation, internships in both government and corporate occupations might be created. Here, students would learn how to perform various occupational tasks by actually doing them. They would spend three months, for example, learning the skills and attributes of one position, then move on to another occupation, thereby covering six or so different job possibilities over a two-year period. Not only would they learn how to perform different types of work, but they would also spend time on the job critically evaluating the work they were doing, both from the perspective of what that job contributed to the larger economy of American society, as well as the kinds of problems workers had to face in completing their assigned tasks. Possible changes in the work place would thus be broached, including a discussion of alternative manufacturing possibilities.

In the government sector, alternative ways of better serving the public would be discussed, along with ways of circumventing bureaucratic red tape. Funding priorities might be considered as well. These discussions would take the form of seminars held with on-the-job personnel and high school instructors. At the end of a given internship, students might be expected to write a critical evaluation of their job placement, including recommendations for changes in goals of production as well as types of production. These papers would then be turned over to full-time employees who supervised their particular internship to make use of as best they could in improving their own situation. The end result of such an internship process would be to make students better able to choose possible employment, give them a good critical evaluation of problems in the marketplace and government service, and possibilities for what might be done to change these occupational tasks. It would also give students a feeling that their evaluations are important for improving the quality of life and work in American society.

An extension of this kind of internship would be to incorporate large-scale exchanges of students, both within the United States and with other nations. Here, students might carry on many of the same functions as with their other internships, only they would be doing so in a different region of the nation or world. By spending time in other areas of the country or in other parts of the world, students would be able to gain a knowledge of cultural differences in ways of going about accomplishing different tasks. They might spend time in seminars critically comparing governmental service and economic programs within different regions. They would also begin to get a sense of national problems and a feeling for how the whole nation forms an interdependent whole.

221

Interdisciplinary courses similar to those developed at the elementary school level might also be made a part of high school curriculums. Studies of math, biology, psychology and sociology might focus around specific issues which students were concerned with, both discussing the problem as well as enabling students to become involved in possible solutions. In this way, chemistry would become more than a lab course; rather it would have to consider the impact of chemical developments on such social problems as smog and water pollution. The basics would not be ignored but rather would be encompassed under broader, more interesting course offerings which motivated students to learn the fundamentals in order to solve problems they felt were important.

Above all, students would be taken seriously. They would be given a meaningful role to play both in the development of a new curriculum and in putting such a curriculum into practice. Their interest in sex and intimate relationships would not be shunted aside under the pretense that it does not exist, but rather would be incorporated into the curriculum. It might be possible, for example, to set up youth apartments in which young couples could live together at the same time as they were involved in completing their high school education. In fact, such living situations would be viewed as classes and integrated into the high school subject matter.

Sound farfetched? Perhaps. But think of the money we are now wasting on unwanted pregnancies, on controlling delinquency, on supporting teenage unwed mothers, and for school vandalism. Might not that money be better spent on a school curriculum which prevented these problems from occurring?

Who will bring this curriculum about? Parents, alarmed over the truancy rate of their offspring, might be motivated to put pressure on school boards and school principals to try an alternative. Teachers, frustrated by empty classrooms and students who never do their homework because they can't "get into it", might also be willing to try out some of the suggestions briefly outlined above. Beyond parents and teachers, however, students would be prime candidates to bring about the change process, and indeed, if change is to be successful, students must be a part of any new curricular design. The reason for this is readily apparent. If it is not "their" program, then why should they support it? How do they know it's not just another one of those top-down directives they have already experienced throughout their educational career? If the problem with existing curriculum has become a personal problem for students, then they must be able to deal with this problem, at least partially, themselves.

Yet how can students change a curriculum that has existed for decades? Students have far more power than they realize. Public school budgets are determined by school attendance. The already high absenteeism rate at many high schools has caused a great deal of concern, as have test scores indicating that students are not learning the basics as well as their parents did. The threat of massive student strikes or boycotts thus gives students a great deal of leverage in attempting to transform school curriculums.

Their low reading, writing, and math scores also enable them to tell school authorities that existing course offerings are not working, not because students are less intelligent than before, but because such course offerings do not address student interest and needs. Students might receive encouragement and insight into how to go about changing curriculum from the new professionals we spoke about in the previous chapter, the truant officers who will help youth understand the cause of their absenteeism, the juvenile court judge and probation officer who will show them how to gain more power to deal with problems causing their criminal behavior, the high school counselor and teacher who sees what the difficulty is and wants to try out a more viable alternative.

Changes in curriculum are not a one-shot campaign. Rather, students must use their new power to transform the high school governance structure, to give themselves some degree of parity in future curricular matters, and in other issues facing the school. Only when high school students come to see the school they attend as *their* community, will they be willing to become responsible for what transpires within its walls.

III

College and university curriculums need to be drastically altered as well. Perhaps the easiest place to begin is within existing academic departments. Here, courses should be shifted from a passive to an active orientation, that is, they should deal with solving specific questions or problems. For example, the psychology department might offer a course called *Identity Crises and What To Do About Them.* The meteorology department might offer a course called *The Effect of Pollution on Urban Problems.*

Beyond specific course changes, departments might begin to offer four or five course concentrations in solving specific problems. For example, the political science department might have a series of offerings dealing with the problem of increasing citizen participation in electoral politics. Such offerings might focus on why political participation is worthwhile, and what specific groups might gain from greater participation. Electoral reforms could also be considered, and students might spend time in the field attempting to bring about changes in the electoral system. One term paper could be required which covered all five courses, serving to integrate these courses, as well as relating classroom discussions with community involvement. A student might be required to take all of the coursework dealing with a specific set of issues in a single semester, thereby permitting him to expend his full energies and time on a specific problem.

But the breakdown of knowledge into academic departments or disciplines, as we noted in Chapter 2, is not only outdated, but it is philosophically bankrupt as well. Accordingly, departments need to be disbanded and curriculum realigned along an interdisciplinary perspective, based on resolution of specific questions or problems. For example, a member of the sociology department might join faculty from economics, urban planning, history and political science to form a curriculum which deals with the problem of poverty – what causes it, and how can it be solved? Along these same lines, faculty from geography, meteorology, biology, chemistry and sociology might form an interdisciplinary curriculum around the problem of smog.

Again, these curriculums might encompass a student's entire semester's work, that is, the student would invest all of his time in dealing with the problem of poverty or smog. The following semester, he or she would enroll in another problem-centered area. Such a curriculum does not sacrifice knowledge for relevance; rather, it has the student learn much of what they were traditionally taught within a more interesting, integrated, and practical framework. Accordingly, a student dealing with the problem of poverty would be able to learn how different aspects of sociology are applicable to working with this issue. What do social theorists have to say about the relationship of poverty to the larger society? How would a social researcher investigate the causes of poverty and the ramifications for poverty victims? How is family communication affected by economic conditions? Similarly, a student would learn political theory by examining the role poor people play in political struggles; how political apathy is related to poverty; how Congress has dealt with the "underclass".

A problem-centered, interdisciplinary curriculum would have students go outside the university to spend a specified number of hours each week working on analyzing a given problem, or on attempting to solve it. This would also mean that part of any interdisciplinary faculty would be made up of persons already working in the field. For example, a social worker and a representative of a welfare rights organization might join the faculty in a curriculum dealing with poverty. Nor would welfare recipients be excluded from becoming part of the teaching staff. Having students devote their full energies to dealing with one general issue in a semester or quarter alleviates problems of fragmentation and eliminates fifty-minute class periods.

The students also come to feel that they are a part of a research team making a valuable contribution to society, that their education is a legitimate occupation, one which society must take seriously. This in turn encourages the student to invest more time and energy in the curriculum in which they are enrolled. No longer are they aimless youth, going to college because there's nothing else to do.

This type of curriculum would also enable faculty to focus their research on interdisciplinary and practical issues, thus giving them greater respectability in the eyes of the general public. As inquiry into one problem area became less necessary, faculty might re-form into different interdisciplinary teams, thus permitting maximum flexibility in subject matter development.

Such an interdisciplinary curriculum is not restricted to immediate problems facing the community or urban setting of which the university is a part. Rather, interdisciplinary curriculums might be created around more theoretical problems causing interest among faculty and students. What is the meaning of existence when each of us must die? What is the relationship between ESP and the design of our solar system? A faculty composed of philosophers, astronomers, psychologists, sociologists, and biologists might form to deal with these issues.

Beyond these changes in curriculum, we might begin to see the university as a living laboratory, an alternative model of American society, a place where new forms of governance, new ways of relating, and different types of economic systems are woven into a social curriculum. The creation of such a university would reverse the long-established dictum that education should reflect society. Instead, it would provide a new type of education which questions existing values, challenges traditional ways of doing things and traditional organizational patterns. Students would learn by working in the "alternative society", by sharing in its governance system, and by attempting to solve problems the society encounters.

How might these changes in the university be brought about? How can faculty be convinced to give up their vested interests in specific disciplines and departments? As in high schools, students possess a great deal of latent power. Colleges and universities only stay in business if students continue to enroll in their programs. Equally, many professors place their jobs in jeopardy if no one shows up for their classes, if lecture halls stay vacant and unattended. Students can use their enrollment power to force universities to change the orientation of their curriculum. Specific departments might be picked out as "test" cases, with suggestions being offered for the creation of experimental, interdisciplinary, problem-oriented curriculums. Nor need departments and faculty be approached from a confrontational mode of operation. Rather, it can be pointed out that the world is more accurately and effectively portrayed from an interdisciplinary perspective, thus adding to the quality of teaching, as well as the quality of research undertaken by particular faculty members.

But how can students organize collectively if they have never been shown how? An initial goal of even a small group of students who push for changes in curriculum might be the creation of a class designed to implement these very changes. Such a course might be titled *Educational Change* and students would use their class time to review existing curriculum, make recommendations, and attempt to get these recommendations adopted by various departments. Sympathetic faculty members might be approached to teach this class. Faculty advisors might also broach the possibility of curricular alternatives with students who come to them for assistance. Other techniques such a class might employ would include research into how recent graduates have applied knowledge gleaned through academic coursework, as well as petitions and rallies to gain support for their position.

Student government, an organization typically concerned with extracurricular activities might also be persuaded to become involved in more curricular matters. Slates of students might run for office on the basis of changes they would desire in university course offerings and the way such courses are taught, as well as in the present university governance structure. An active campaign of three or four slates making various recommendations concerning the direction the university ought to go would do a great deal to give students a respected voice in campus policy-making, preparing the way for consideration of the university as an alternative community composed of faculty, students and administrators, each of whom has a say in how the campus will be run, and what the goals of the university should be.

Faculty organizations such as the AFT, AAUP and academic senate might also be approached by students and interested faculty to consider major revisions in curriculum and departmental structure.

Ultimately, changes in the university must be brought about by students, faculty and administrators who see the causes of their own coping behavior as lying within the curriculum and governance structure. Instead of viewing student apathy and boredom as the student's problem, the question becomes, *What is there about the organization of the university that generates these symptoms, and how can this situation be transformed?*

Creating An Alternative Economy: Goods and Skills Exchanges

15

One of the reasons we are powerless is because we are isolated in apartments and housing tracts, protecting our individuality, our personal space, by a wall of material appendages which we erect around us. Finding ourselves in alienating jobs, we seek compensation in new wardrobes, cars, and other technological gadgets which we stockpile in our living quarters, often using these as a way of defining our lives as worthwhile and purposeful. But, as we noted, in Chapter 4, such superfluous consumption rarely leads to the kind of meaningful existence we hope for. Rather, it keeps us on a never-ending consumer treadmill. It is also costly. In fact, the necessity of paying our BankAmericard, Master Card and other monthly credit obligations often means that we must continue to hold employment in unsatisfactory jobs. How are we to break this coping cycle?

While many of us are not interested in altering our consumer behavior, we ARE willing to pursue policies which will save us some amount of money. The creation of a goods exchange in our apartment complex or housing tract is a viable place to begin. A quick look in our bedroom closet will reveal a wide variety of clothing which we rarely wear. In our kitchens there are pots and plates and gadgets we once thought would save us time and energy, but now lie on back shelves covered with dust. In our garages are hand and power tools which we start up about once a year, leaving them safely tucked away the rest of the time on workshop tables and metal shelves. Since we rarely use many of these items, it would be possible to loan them out without causing any unnecessary hardship to ourselves or our families. In return, we might be able to borrow something which we might temporarily need, rather than rushing off to a nearby shopping center to obtain the item in question. Yet how do we know what other people own and would be willing to loan out? A goods exchange is a way of answering this question.

Such an exchange might begin by getting everyone in a given apartment complex or on a block to list items they would be willing to share. Initially, these might be things we could just as well do without, dresses we rarely wear, tools we never use, plastic dishes the Avon lady sold us. Someone on the block then collects all the lists and categorizes them by type or item, and makes a small directory. For example:

Dresses	Name	
Size 7, blue, short	*Mary Smith*	*222-3333*
Size 9, green, low cut	*Sandy Stevens*	*444-5555*
Records	**Name**	
Beatles, Hard Days Night	*Terry Timmons*	*999-1010*

Children might also be encouraged to participate in the exchange by listing old bicycles, toys, and books they no longer use. Each member of the Exchange might be expected to put in $5 a month as "insurance" to cover potential damage to an item loaned out, if a dress was stained, or a record scratched or broken. Any time we needed something, we would simply consult our exchange directory, call the person who owned the article that we needed to borrow, and arrange for picking up and returning the item. New commodities could be constantly added to the exchange directory as members grew more used to loaning things out and getting them back in one piece.

II

Many of us not only have closets full of clothes we rarely wear, but we also have skills we have developed as hobbies over the years. Coming home from work in the evening we like to go out to the garage and tinker with our cars, fix our television sets, or put a new coat of paint on the house. In fact, we often take more pride in the skills we put to use outside of work than those we use on our job. We also tend to feel that our accomplishments at home are more significant; we can see the final product of our labor.

Though we are proficient at performing certain skills at home, there are many other things we don't know how to do, tasks which need to get done, but which we must pay a repairman to accomplish for us. With built-in technological obsolescence, it is not uncommon to have our washer or dryer break down, our car stop functioning, or the plumbing go haywire. Many of the gadgets we purchase simply don't last very long, for if they did, few of us would need to keep coming back for newer replacements.

But repairs can be costly. Suppose we were to add to our Goods Exchange Directory a Skills Exchange. Again, everyone in an apartment complex or on a given block would be asked to list the kinds of skills they felt competent in doing, and these would be categorized in the directory. For example:

Auto Repair	Name	
VW's	*Jim Smith*	*345-6789*
Fords	*Sheri Jones*	*123-9876*

Electrical Repairs	Name	
	Bob Burton	*654-9832*

Skills which could be listed would not be limited to technological areas, but rather might encompass anything from babysitting to massage to teaching pottery to giving piano or French lessons. The next time the television set broke down, we would simply consult the Skills part of our directory for someone who listed television repair, call them up, and work out an exchange, promising to do their laundry, give two pottery lessons, or trim their lawn in return. No money is involved, nor are skills rated by the amount nominally charged by a professional. Rather, the exchange is strictly dependent on the type of agreement reached between the two parties concerned.

Barter systems are, of course, not a new idea. However, they have gained a recent resurgence in this country, owing largely to the high rate of inflation. Informal agreements are typically worked out between immediate neighbors to borrow tools, to watch each other's kids when we go to the movies, though more formalized babysitting cooperatives are becoming common. On the West Coast, Swap-A-Skills are springing up in a wide variety of neighborhoods, and Swap Meets are frequently held at Flea Markets or drive-in movie theaters on weekends.

Goods and Skills exchanges do more than save us money, however. They begin to bring us into contact with our neighbors over commonly shared problems. Though we may not work at similar jobs, we do share the same residential neighborhood, or the same apartment complex. Though we may not be in agreement as to the kinds of things we like to do in our leisure time, we do agree on the high cost of living; the items we own typically break down regardless of our different intellectual and occupational interests. Our kids do go to the same schools. As we begin to exchange skills and goods we begin to get a feeling for who lives in the neighborhood. Perhaps they are not a threat to our identity, after all. Stereotypes begin to break down. The Skills Exchange forces us to have conversations with "unknown" members of our street or apartment building; it forces us to get to know them as we watch them take a look at our dryer, ask them to have a beer, go over to their house to give them some advice on how to get rid of the crabgrass in their lawn. Without money to act as a go-between, we are forced to interact face to face.

Soon, we look forward to helping others with our skills. They are far more appreciative than the corporations we work for, or the public service bureaucracies we serve in. In fact, we can't even remember a time when our supervisor said: *"Thanks a lot for doing a great job".* We begin to feel we are making a worthwhile contribution. We are also saving money. After the goods and skills exchange has functioned for a while, someone suggests we all go in on a paint compressor together and then help each other paint our houses. If we all put in a weekend we could easily do one house. So we buy a compressor. Someone else suggests setting up a food co-op. We could all put in a couple of dollars a week and one of us could go to a wholesaler and see how many crates of fruits and vegetables we could pick up. The food could all be brought back to one of our garages and divided equally. Yeah, we think, why not? A different person could be selected each time to go out and purchase the groceries and different people could rotate dividing it into equal shares and bagging it for pick-up.

Soon our success on our block leads us to think that maybe we should expand a little bit, bring in another twenty or thirty families, people who have skills we don't have. We remember driving past someone's house two blocks away and discovering that they actually had an arc welder in their garage. Imagine that! So we work on expanding the directory and in a short while, we have a hundred families listed. Some of us, however, begin to get booked up in advance, because we have skills, like car repair, which are very much in demand. So we tell people who call us: *"Hey, we'd really like to give you a hand, but we're already overloaded, how about calling someone else?"* Only the other people who repair cars are as busy as we are. Maybe the Skills Exchange wasn't such a good idea after all.

We decide to call a meeting of the entire Exchange membership. We haven't had a meeting before, because everything was accomplished by going door to door to get people involved. Most of the members show up for the meeting because it is held on a Sunday afternoon, and we've blocked off the street and brought out barbecues and a few gallons of wine. It feels good seeing all these people together, people who we only saw as isolated individuals before. We begin to get a sense of community, as if we were living in a small town like the kind we sometimes see on television.

How are we going to solve the problem of too many people needing a particular skill? Suppose, someone says, we begin to have classes on Saturday mornings to teach people how to repair their cars. Whatever cars need to be repaired that day could be brought over to one person's house and the mechanics in the neighborhood could show them what to do. In exchange for teaching people how to repair their cars in the morning, students might devote an afternoon to helping the mechanics out with some particular project. In the future, whenever there seems to be a greater need for some service than there are people to fulfill that need, then such a teaching program should be considered.

Soon after the first meeting a problem develops at the elementary school our children attend. The school is over-crowded, and the playground space is being eaten up by temporary bungalows to house the influx of new children. We have never thought about doing anything involving the school before, but as we listen to our children's complaints, we begin to think of telling the school principal what we think of the matter. Yet, we are only one parent, why should she listen to us? Besides, there's probably nothing she can do anyhow. She can't just ask the last hundred kids who enrolled at the school to find an education elsewhere. But our kids are not the only ones affected by the shrinking playground space. Probably everyone on our block has kids who are complaining about the same thing. Maybe we ought to call a meeting of the Exchange to discuss the problem and figure out what we might be able to do about it?

After a few phone calls we find that we were right, and that other parents are listening to similar complaints. The meeting in our living room is packed. Someone points out that expanding school enrollment is due to the construction of hundreds of new homes in the area without paying any attention to the need for a new school. Perhaps a building moratorium should be placed on the area until such a new school is designed and completed? Maybe we should approach the city council? It is our first meeting to discuss a problem not directly related to the skills and goods exchange. More will follow as we discover the lack of any park facility nearby and other issues directly affecting the neighborhood.

As we become more involved in applying our skills and sharing some of the goods we own, we begin to think about having the exchange go in on larger projects which would benefit the neighborhood. There is a vacant lot nearby which might be purchased collectively by the Exchange. On the lot we could set up a community garden, build a community crafts center, a community laundromat, a cooperative market. If we all shared the cost, the purchase price would not be prohibitive. If we all helped in the construction, it could be done in no time. We suddenly realize that we have begun to change. We have begun to gain control over our lives; we have found something worthwhile to do with ourselves.

This change in attitude begins to be reflected in how we approach our job. As the exchange has developed, we have found that we do not need as much money to live on; we have also found that we can practice skills during our leisure time at home which are more meaningful to us than those we perform at work. As a result, we have become less dependent on our occupation as both a source of income and as a source of personal satisfaction.

Perhaps in the not-too-distant future we might only have to work half-time. In fact, some of the people in the neighborhood have been talking about job-sharing, where three people share two full-time positions. It could be suggested where we work, as well. As our dependence on occupation is reduced, we feel more free to criticize company policies. At some of our neighborhood meetings we have discovered that many other people are faced with the same job problems we have, and we have even spent some time discussing what might be done to improve our occupational situations. In fact, after telling our supervisor what we thought of the way tasks were being performed, and suggesting improvements, we couldn't wait to get home and tell some of the other guys on the street, because we know they will support us, just as we will support them. If we get laid off, maybe they'll even find something for us to do where they work.

As we begin to practice meaningful skills in the community, we are also put into contact with other women, women who work and must also put meals on the table, do the dishes and laundry. We begin to discuss ways of getting our husbands to change their attitudes toward what we do, the "two jobs" we hold. For those of us employed full time in our homes, we begin to use the exchange to get free time to go back to school, or to take up other interests. Instead of seeing ourselves as being stuck in the suburbs, or in our apartment, we begin to feel as if we are a functional part of a community, that we too are making a valid contribution through the skills we perform. We begin to take up carpentry and plumbing, put in energy investigating local problems, setting up committees within the Exchange to make sure the work is evenly distributed and that it gets done.

At first, the exchange of goods was an interesting idea, a way for us not to feel so guilty every time we looked in our closet and discovered the amount of stuff we had accumulated over the years which we never used. But we were still watching television ads, we still felt the urge to go out and buy something new; to cope with a meaningless existence. Yet, as the Exchange has developed, we notice that we do not watch as much television; in fact, most television programs seem bland in comparison to the things we have become involved in on our block. The skills and goods directory has been expanded to include courses people are giving in their homes, and to the listing of interests people would like to share. One couple gets a lot of enjoyment out of going to foreign films and discussing them afterward, and wonders if anyone else in the neighborhood has similar tastes. Another couple goes skiing; a third wants to set up a weekly volleyball game; a fourth wants to put together a neighborhood orchestra; a fifth wants to know if anyone would like to discuss ESP; a sixth wants to get into transcendental meditation. Others have cabins, boats and campers they'd be willing to loan out, and backpacking trips they'd like to organize.

With so many things going on, we hardly have time to make it over to see what's on sale at the Mall. Nor do we feel the need to do so, because we have suddenly found that we can have a worthwhile identity without having to buy one. The transition was so natural; the more involved in the neighborhood we became, the less we thought about how we "looked", the less we thought about maintaining our individuality and status as defined by Madison Avenue. But we haven't given up our individuality either, only now we express ourselves by the contributions we are making to others in the neighborhood, and are rewarded by the contributions they make to us. Instead of replacing our consumer coping behavior with another coping mechanism, we have begun to confront identity problems which caused us to cope in the first place.

III

Our involvement in the Exchange has also given us a sense of power which we did not have before, and which we used to seek vicariously in the actions of professional athletes and movie stars. This power leads us to expand the Exchange in other directions. We begin to set up a neighborhood newsletter which discusses common problems affecting Exchange members, upcoming events, and pros and cons of purchasing different items for the use of all Exchange members. Some of us who have dropped down to half-time work begin to think about setting up neighborhood cooperatively run businesses, producer cooperatives which supply necessary goods and services to those living inside, as well as outside the neighborhood. Someone suggests setting up a gas station/garage; others talk about a drug store; still others want to experiment with specific application of solar heating for the average home.

Several computer specialists in the neighborhood discuss the idea of putting computer terminals in their homes and setting up information retrieval systems for use by the average consumer. For example, if someone wants to find out what has been written about a particular problem or topic, the question they were concerned with could be fed into the computer. There is mention of setting up a neighborhood credit union and possibly a bank, which could both fund these producer cooperatives and lend money to Exchange members at low interest.

Involvement in banks and credit unions would require a greater membership than our Exchange presently holds. Yet, as the Exchange has been developing, other neighborhoods have heard about it and have begun to organize along similar lines. It may be possible to create an Exchange Federation which could help finance things like credit unions and banks, since they would have thousands of member contributions to draw from. Each neighborhood exchange could send a representative to this central organization, who would articulate the views of their particular neighborhood, participate in discussions, and then report back to their neighborhood unit.

The Exchange Federation could draw up specific action proposals, which would then have to be voted on by everyone belonging to each neighborhood cooperative. Here, economic and political power would begin to emerge, as exchange members discovered that not only did they have a say in how *their* producer cooperatives were run, and the kinds of commodities or services they would supply, but also in decisions which affected other aspects of their lives as well. Such an Exchange Federation could run people for school board positions, for city council seats, and could lobby with local legislators and Congressmen and women for specific bills which would deal with problems directly affecting their neighborhoods.

But the Exchange Federation would maintain voting power in the hands of individual members, thereby strengthening participatory democracy. Politics would no longer seem like a distant interest, as something news-casters mentioned once in a while on television, nor would power to deal with local economic decisions be divorced from power to deal with pressing social problems.

In a similar sense, apartment renters might use Goods and Skills Exchanges to first save money, then to organize tenant unions which could deal with needed apartment repairs and high rents. They could then focus on the development of neighborhood credit unions and explore the possibility of purchasing the buildings in which they lived, running them as cooperatively owned, multi-unit dwellings. Here, too, we might find those having trouble dealing with the owner of one apartment seeking support from nearby tenant unions whose strength was greater.

Producer cooperatives might be expected to form around new kinds of occupations, rather than duplicating what already exists. Alternative medical centers might be developed along the lines suggested in Chapter 13. At these centers, doctors and lay persons would begin to focus on the social problems causing physical disease, mental illness, drug and alcohol abuse. As these causes were pinpointed, that is, as the structure and organization of the community was examined to see what there was about the way it functioned that might have generated these ailments and coping mechanisms, specific recommendations could be made, and Exchange membership meetings called to act on them. In cases where social action was necessary to deal with specific types of occupational alienation, found outside the neighborhood or jurisdiction of the Federated Exchange, the close working network of exchange members could provide groups to carry out specific change strategies, or might at least provide support for individual members who risked their jobs to change their occupational situation.

The Exchange might also become involved in bringing about a school curriculum which matched the direction in which neighborhoods were moving. The student-centered, social problems-oriented curriculum proposed in the last chapter might easily tie in with the development of neighborhood power. Instead of splitting young people off from their parents, both could work together on dealing with specific problems. As children grew used to sharing toys, repairing bicycles, and exchanging skills on their block, this sense of cooperation could be expanded into the classroom setting to deal with more academic subjects, basic learning skills, and problem solving.

High school students might find apprenticeships within the new producer cooperatives starting up, or might learn basic fix-it skills and organizing strategies by taking "classes" in nearby neighborhoods. College and university students might return to their communities to experiment with new ideas, new ways of relating and communicating, and new non-polluting technologies. In return, Exchange members might enroll in institutes of higher learning to gain further knowledge which they could then bring back and share with their neighbors. As such, education would come to be viewed as a life-long process, rather that attendance at a specific school for a specified period of time.

Other professionals might also use their neighborhoods as a base from which to launch a new perspective of society. Alternative ways of dealing with crime could be explored, with "facilitators" taking the place of police to control neighborhood disturbances. As people discovered that they could borrow what they needed, crime would probably decrease, especially burglary. Middle class delinquency would also be reduced as youth came to discover that they had power to deal with their school situation and were supported in their efforts by parents who treated their activities as worthwhile involvements which should be taken seriously. They would also find meaningful roles to play in their own neighborhoods, and among people who respected the contributions they were making. As individuals came to feel that they "owned" their communities, they would begin to identify crime as a social rather than a personal problem.

Exchange Federations might begin to focus in on changes in television programming and on advertising as well. As individuals discover that they no longer need the many superfluous commondities produced each year, they would also grow weary of those who try to sell them. Exchange newsletters might have information columns discussing different types of false advertising, products which frequently tended to break down, relationships which did not happen because of the purchase of a specific commodity, men who did not become men because they bought a new sportscoat, as well as evaluating the need to buy superfluous products in the first place. Action items could be brought up at Exchange meetings, suggesting boycotts of specific products felt detrimental to the health of the community. Picket lines might even be formed around stores carrying such brands. Other kinds of consumer action could be suggested also, such as lobbying for the production of durable consumer goods — appliances which rarely broke down, and solar-powered cars.

The development of neighborhood exchanges would be a large step in ending our coping behavior. As we came to see that other people faced many of the same problems we do, we would also come to understand that many of our problems are social rather than personal in nature, and that they can only be solved by working with others, rather than attempting to cope in isolation.

Organizing the Outcasts: The Poor, The Old, The Unemployed

16

Goods and Skills exchanges might be expected to be of particular benefit to the poor, the old, and the unemployed. While members of this group lack money and employment, the sharing of goods and skills would provide a more adequate way of surviving in the short run, and a way of organizing to gain power for a better livelihood in the long run. Though they may own few surplus commodities, the sharing of what they do have may be a beginning. Many among the poor have skills, particularly those who have been forced into retirement, and would welcome the opportunity to contribute their knowledge if they felt it was going for a worthwhile goal, or if they knew they would receive an equal contribution in return.

Yet, there are fundamental differences between the poor and the middle class, as well as significant variance within the ranks of the poor themselves. Some persons may be poor because they have never been able to get a good-paying job; others may be poor because they have grown too old to keep up with their peers in a sales force and have been forced into unemployment; still others, particularly non-white, minority youth, have never been able to find any employment at all. While the middle class copes with alienating work by purchasing superflouous consumer goods, the poor cope with unemployment and poverty by making do as best they can; by focusing on status symbols within their own subcultures or by becoming listless and unmotivated, seeing no chance to improve their situation, and unwilling to share in available coping mechanisms—drugs, crime, prostitution. Though the poor and the middle class differ in their economic condition, they both look to the same material goods for salvation—the middle class because they see these goods as a way of dealing with conditions of alienating work, boring schools, and inadequate relationships — the poor because they see these goods as improving their status, giving them a larger piece of the pie, and making their lives easier. Regardless, the middle class have access to these goods, and the poor do not.

How, then, can the poor, the aged, and the unemployed confront and solve problems which directly affect their lives?

I

What kind of power do we have if we are living in a condition of poverty? Unlike the middle class, we lack economic power. If we refused to purchase consumer goods, few people will know the difference. If we withhold our services from employment in corporations or government bureaucracies, it will have no impact because we are not working, or if we are, it is at unskilled, low-paying jobs for which we can only too easily be replaced. We do have political power, however. We can still vote, we can distribute petitions, we can hold rallies, we can walk precincts for specific candidates, and we can ourselves run for political office. Through our votes on specific issues or in support of specific candidates we can attempt to influence legislation, changing government spending priorities so that we can get a larger share of the action—money for worthwhile jobs, better housing, better medical care, better schools, for building a better community.

But such power is a long way off. Unlike our middle class brethren, we are resistant to group organizing efforts not so much because we want to protect our individuality, but rather because we are afraid, afraid we will be cut off of welfare, afraid we will lose our unemployment benefits, and afraid they will fire us from the low paying jobs we now hold and because we have no alternative employment. We are also leery because such organizing efforts have never worked in the past and because we have already sacrificed enough. Moreover, how do we know these new efforts would prove any different? How do we know someone is not just trying to take advantage of us again, gather our votes, then leave us to fend for ourselves; manipulate and trick us into supporting empty promises? It has happened before; it will happen again. And even if we wanted to organize, how could we begin? Whom can we trust? Who will lead us?

First, we must change our attitude. We must come to see poverty as a problem because of the way the society in which we live is organized. While it is a problem for us as well, we are not to blame, nor can we, by our own, isolated, individual action do much to change the conditions we and our families must presently confront. Again, we can begin with the coping mechanisms many of us now use; we might also demand help from professionals when we come to their attention, when our coping mechanisms get out of hand. As we noted in Chapter 13, drug abuse counselors can help us examine the conditions which caused us to become involved in drug usage in the first place. They can help organize us into groups, showing us how to draft legislation and lobby for change. If they do not want to, then we can ask and demand that they fulfill the obligations of their job. One of the initial tasks we must deal with is to get those who would assist us to see our many problems as related, rather than piecemeal. We are not just hooked on heroin, and shifting to methadone will not be enough. Rather, we are also unemployed, nor are there jobs available which promise a substantial increase in income. We are unemployed and we lack an education that relates to our lives and will help us advance in terms of salary and living conditions. Accordingly, drug abuse counselors must also work with unemployment counselors and with the police and with social workers and school teachers, since not one of our problems can be solved without dealing with all of them. Nor need such a professional task force come from the ranks of the middle class.

In fact, it is probably presumptuous of us to think that one will. The first new jobs we must demand in exchange for helping elect particular candidates to office is funding for our own drug counselors, alcoholic advisors, police who will act as facilitators for resolution of problems which led us to commit crimes, and social workers who view welfare as a symptom, and who would work with us to gain a bigger share of the public and private budget. Nor need we wait for funding, since many of us who are unemployed could begin to assume these roles right now. There is nothing stopping us.

As we begin to change the attitudes of those who are most susceptible, those so strung out in their coping behavior that their very survival is dependent on such a change—drug addicts, alcoholics, and those facing long prison sentences—we can also begin to affect others in their coping behavior as well, those in line to become the next addicts, alcoholics, and criminals. Here we begin to work with welfare mothers and men on unemployment; with school counselors dealing with chronic truants; and with community mental health therapists dealing with the severely depressed. We also visit old age homes and senior centers, talking with the aged about the problems they face and what might be done about them, attempting to show them that the position they now find themselves in is not their fault, but rather the symptom of a system which has no use for them. As it is important to see the relationship between drug addiciton, unemployment, and poor housing, it is equally important to begin to see persons classified within these categories as sharing common problems—the need to cope—rather than treating them as distinct problem groups. One of the ways poor people are kept powerless, in fact, is by their fragmentation into various social service agency categories, depending upon the particular malady they are analyzed as suffering from.

Not only must drug addicts, alcoholics, and the unemployed begin to see themselves as sharing a common problem, but age groups must make an effort to get over similar differences. An in-depth look at the problems facing seniors and youth reveals many common concerns. Both groups are essentially powerless, lacking worthwhile employment, and many of the consumer goods that go along with it. Neither group is treated with respect by the age group in power, those 21-55 who hold steady, well-paying jobs and live in expensive apartments, condominiums, and housing tracts. In a society placing a high value on technological knowledge and expertise, neither youth nor seniors are considered worthy of esteem. Unfortunately, most youth view their elders with the same disdain as their parents, for seniors represent wrinkles, sickness and death, and most youth, despite their current predicament, feel they have their whole lives in front of them, so why should they concern themselves with problems of old age now? And yet, both groups can benefit by aligning with each other around certain issues.

II

Once we have grown used to the idea that the problems we are faced with are social, rather than personal in character, we must begin to develop strategies for changing the social conditions which are keeping us poor and unemployed, and which force us to use coping mechanisms which do little for our situation.

We must begin to think about organizing collectively, to give each other support, as well as to give ourselves greater power. This is especially important when we think about quitting some of the coping habits we have developed, for it is not enough that we are ending our reliance on drugs; rather, our habit helps support an entire drug network—pushers, suppliers, manufacturers—who will do their utmost to keep us from quitting. Only if we have group support will our efforts prove successful. How do we organize collectively? What goals should we seek to achieve?

The goods and skills exchange mentioned in the last chapter represents one such effort. Once we bring people together and become accustomed to sharing skills and goods, we can begin to tackle neighborhood problems, and eventually become involved in the political process in much the same way as we discussed. There are other places we can begin, as well. Since we are all renters, often of dilapidated housing, we might form a tenants' union demanding improved living conditions and lower rents. But, if this is the only place we have to live, most of us would be reluctant to become involved in such an association for fear of finding ourselves with no place to go. What other resources do we have available? Well, we have time on our hands. If we are reluctant to share skills and goods, at least initially, and a rent strike appears too risky, then perhaps we should begin elsewhere. Perhaps what we should first attempt to do is get people to see that they are faced with common problems. We should call a general meeting, at a nearby church or hall. But how do we get everyone there? First, we must find out who people respect in the neighborhood, who they will listen to, the informal leaders. If we can get them involved, they might make lists of issues which they see as affecting everyone in *their* neighborhood, circulating these on leaflets, making phone calls, seeing people on the street, urging them to attend. Another starting point may be at a school our kids go to, through a PTA meeting; or we might talk to people who hang out at community or senior centers.

Once we have gotten everyone together, we might try to figure out the three or four problems that are on everyone's mind, the things they think most about, and what they see as possible solutions to their problems. After a general airing of views it will probably become apparent that most people in our neighborhood tend to be troubled by the same things. We focus in on what seems to be the major complaint—lack of jobs. Now how do we get more jobs? Either we must put pressure on government leaders and private corporations to create more jobs, or we must demonstrate that there is work to be done right here in our neighborhood which the government or private corporations should be willing to pay to have completed. How can we pressure government leaders when they don't seem to care about what happens to us? We could refuse to vote for them and instead support candidates pledged to help us out. Again, we have time on our hands, time to do door-to-door canvassing, time to talk to people, time to get petitions circulated, and to walk picket lines. We are affected by problems of unemployment; who else is? There are fifty of us in the room. How many others living in the city might find common cause with us? How many others are living at or below the poverty line, how many others are unemployed? There are thousands of unemployed youth; there are also senior citizens who were forced into retirement and would just as soon be working. If we make contact with them and agree to work together around this issue, it will make for a lot of votes. The problem is that we have never voted together, all of us as a bloc.

Similar meetings take place around the city. We are standing outside the unemployment office, out of work now for eight months. We have no job prospects. We see familiar faces, men and women in similar situations whom we have been competing with for whatever becomes available, though there is nothing. Around Christmas time we notice some of the faces have disappeared, but they are back in January. Hey, how about coming over to my place for a beer so we can talk about what we can do, how we might be able to get jobs for all of us? Or, we are playing bingo with the other older guys down at the center, wishing we were back at the plant, or doing something. There must be some other alternative, we say to the person sitting next to us. I'd like to travel, he replies, but I don't have the money. I'd like to be a carpenter, someone sitting across from us says, but I'd also like to get paid for what I do. Maybe we could figure out a way of getting more money, of finding some decent jobs . . .

Once we figure out the problem we want to initially

focus in on, and other persons who may be willing to support us, we form a coalition. Nor do we have to wait for them to come to us. If seniors are not involved, or youth do not come out of the woodwork, we go to them, using much the same tactics as we used to organize ourselves, working through informal leaders and concentrating on what seems to be a significant problem in their lives. We let them know what we are doing, and show them the potential if all of us work together. We also approach more formal organizations, attempting to figure out what groups are already working for the same goal as we have set for ourselves. Are there any associations whose main consideration is organizing and lobbying for the unemployed? Labor unions? American Association of Retired Persons? Perhaps there are none. We might turn to other groups for possible assistance. The National Lawyers Guild to help us draft legislation. Common Cause. Ralph Nader. We might also put pressure on police, social workers, teachers, community mental health counselors for assistance of the type discussed earlier. Still others may be potential recruits to our cause. High school and college age youth not currently seeking employment but who may be doing so in the near future might wish to join our ranks, since they may be faced with many of the same unemployment problems we are currently grappling with. In fact, this topic may already be a part of the new curriculum mentioned in Chapter 14, and might form the focal point for a semester's work.

We formalize our association, naming it Citizens for Better Employment. We divide the coalition into various committees: for example, a committee to research existing legislation on the creation of more jobs, or on the possibility of mandatory job sharing if there are not enough jobs to go around. Another committee explores the possibility of putting a referendum on the next ballot calling for the creation of a specified number of jobs in the community in which we are organizing, rebuilding the central city area, setting up our own clinics, our own stores, our own cooperative housing projects, our own schools, our own industries and service organizations. It is not difficult to come up with a rationale for this enterprise. The committee is able to document how much money is spent annually on police, welfare bureaucracies, unemployment checks, medical services, drug and alcohol counselors, parole officers, and prisons, all of which serve to perpetuate the problem. Might not these same funds be used to support community employment? If the crime rate goes down, might middle class neighborhoods benefit as well? A third committee arranges to have speakers from different government offices dealing with employment address the Citizens for Better Employment organization. Local politicians are also invited and asked why nothing is being done. The research committee is ready with facts and figures on the number of unemployed, the jobs available, and the limits of existing legislation so that political leaders are not allowed to make empty promises, or to say that something is being done, when it is not. They are told that unless they begin to sponsor employment legislation, we will throw our support around someone else during the next election. And, so they get the point, we tell them how many of us there are—200,000 in this city city alone. But they are only one congressperson, they complain, what can they do?

They are partially right. We decide to work on two levels at once, the creation of a statewide employment program, and a national effort. The strategies we adopt for both are similar. We send representatives to other cities in the state to begin organizing similar constituencies. It is easier, because we can show them what we have already done. Already, the state has responded to the pressure we have applied, and given us $100,000 to fund a pilot program and to keep us cooled down. We use the money to staff our headquarters, and to hire our first set of social problem-community oriented counselors. As these other cities organize, they too are able to influence their legislators and congresspersons. We start a statewide newsletter so we can keep in touch. The money we have received gives us the feeling that we are on our way; that if we can stick together something will be accomplished. We begin to make contact with other cities in different parts of the country so as to be able to influence other congresspersons and the President. We create a national newsletter, addressing employment as well as other problems facing the poor. We pick out a list of target congresspersons whom we send massive petitions to, asking for new employment bills.

We form a committee for direct action. They organize rallies and picket lines around federal buildings and state and federal employment agencies. They draw attention to the issue, making local television newscasts; even Dan Rather wants to know what's going on. We take a trip to the state capital to join 20,000 others in a rally, but the governor is "not in" the day we arrive. No matter, we decide to stay and camp out in front of his office. A similar rally is planned for the White House later on.

There is an attempt by some congresspersons to fight back, to arouse middle class taxpayers who might initially bear the brunt of funding programs which will aid us. Where will the additional money come from? they ask. Think of how much you would save if you eliminated our problems, we reply. Then *we* would be out of work, the social workers, police, and drug counselors among them answer back. Then use your current employment to help us now, we tell them; help us campaign for better jobs for everyone; convince those whom you now counsel or arrest to join us in trying to deal with the causes of their problems.

Besides, we tell them, there are other places to get money.What if the defense budget were cut in half, we write our congresspersons, what if we could save 110 billion dollars a year? We might have enough to both employ us and the defense engineers now working for Lockheed, McConnell Douglas, and Boeing, because the money would not be spent on dead-end investments like bombs, new missile systems, and other military hardware. But we could not do that, they write back. Why not? we reply; what has our defense industry done for us, who has it protected us poor people from?

Our effort to organize the unemployed has a great many spin-offs. While we are campaigning on this issue, we find ourselves meeting more frequently with our neighbors, and discussing other problems we share in common. We begin to rely on each other for help and support; we throw neighborhood parties. One of our leaders is taken off of welfare because she has been labeled by the authorities. We rush to her assistance, forming a massive picket line around the Department of Social Services. A lawyer friendly to our cause challenges the Department's action on the grounds of abridgement of First Amendment freedoms—of speech and assembly. They give her back her grant. Many of us begin discussing ways to improve the neighborhood right now without waiting; others of us are making plans for the future, talking about different types of neighborhood government, the location of a free clinic, a cooperative market. Others of us are thinking about enrolling in adult education programs and getting the board of education to set up a community school offering classes particularly geared toward our needs and the needs of the area of the city in which we live. Someone says we should get our own radio station, another, our own television talk show. Hey, why don't we make a movie, we ask, knowing forty or fifty million of us who might turn out to watch it.

17

At some point along the way, the actions we have engaged in will begin to have an impact on the economy. The thousands of goods and skills exchanges we have initiated will begin to take their toll on the profits large corporations will be able to make by selling us superfluous consumer goods. As the demand for such goods decreases, those least able to afford to be laid off—department store clerks —will be given their notices. Yet, the spread of Exchanges will enable those laid off to survive, at least in the short run, by receiving aid and support from the cooperatives which have grown up in their neighborhoods. Soon, retail stores will stop ordering as many new products from manufacturers, who also must begin firing their employees. The demand for plumbers, electricians, and auto mechanics will also begin to drop off, as many of us learn how to repair our own leaky faucets and faulty carbuerators. Unions will be up in arms, unable to find work for their members. At the same time, lobbying and electoral efforts by the coalition of the poor, the unemployed, youth and seniors will force cuts in the defense budget, causing further lay-offs of defense personnel. The unemployment and welfare rolls will begin to rise, causing a crisis in the social service bureaucracy. Where is the money to come from to pay out weekly benefits to all those who need them? The decline in consumer purchases forces the stock market to drop to a record low. Investors are trying desperately to pull their money out before it's too late. Corporate executives and government leaders are in a panic, unable to figure out what to do. They've never had to force people to buy before in order to keep the economy functioning. An emergency session of Congress is convened, the main question before them being: how can we get people to start coping again so our profits will return?

It might not happen this way. Rather, as our attempts to confront and solve our problems reach roadblocks, we discover that fundamental solutions are impossible without changing the orientation and manner in which American society is organized. Since supporting coping lifestyles is a big industry, not only for private corporations which supply superfluous consumer goods, but for social service bureaucracies, police and other professionals who would treat our coping symptoms, the demise of coping behavior spells the end of employment for millions of persons. How are we to employ everyone? Is full employment still necessary if the demand for products and services has decreased? If it is not, then will a few of us work to support the rest of us, or will we all share equally in what needs to get done, but at a greatly reduced work week? If thirty or forty percent of us are out of work, will the kind of profit-oriented economy we have been used to still be possible, and if it is not, then what kind of economy will we replace it with? A planned economy?

It might happen at our place of business when we discover that it is impossible to have meaningful employment unless we can also have a say in what is being produced, and how it is to be produced, and that the people we work for are unwilling to grant us such decision-making power, because then *we* would own the company. It might happen when we begin to practice the new preventive medicine, attempting to eliminate situations which generate excessive stress in our lives. Here, we may run into difficulty as our values begin to conflict with those of large corporations demanding maximum output from their sales personnel, and unable to make a profit unless such output is maintained. It might happen as we become more and more involved in our new educational curricula designed to solve personal and community problems, and we discover that, upon graduation, there is no place for the meaningful lifestyles we have created. There are no occupations which match our social change interests.

There will, of course, be those who attempt to dissuade us of our position, to show us that coping can still be personally rewarding, to offer us new gadgets, better drugs, greater "participation" in our occupational endeavors. And, for awhile, we may succumb to the temptations put before us, to the new slogans, CHANGE AMERICA, BUY A BUICK, to the co-optation of our efforts by those who would use them to make a profit. But if we have come to the conclusion that coping is no longer worth it, then these ploys by the opposition will at worst be momentary setbacks; at best, we will laugh at them for what they are, or grow angry because they represent what we have come to find boring and distasteful.

II

So then it might happen. We would wake up one morning and read that the economy has collapsed. It would not be the end of the world, of American society, only the form that society has taken. Having power, we would realize ultimately means being able to create a society which matches our new values and interests, while coping has meant holding on to a societal organization that fails to satisfy the needs of its members. Nor, would the opportunity to redesign America mean the demise of all of our technological skills and know-how. We peek out of our living room window: how do we create a new social order?

First, we would have to calculate what needs our new society would have to meet: food, clothing, shelter, and medical services for 235 million people. How much would it take per month, how would these be supplied, who would supply them? What problems would our new society have to solve that the old one was unable to? Employment? Meaningful political participation? Pollution? Stress? Crime? Poverty? After some thought and discussion, we come up with the following goals:

1) The development of an economy which is not detrimental to the environment.
2) The development of an economy which guarantees everyone a decent standard of living.

3) The development of an economy which guarantees everyone a job which is challenging and meaningful.

4) The development of an economy where everyone has an equal say in what will be produced, and in other major economic and political decisions.

5) The development of a society which guarantees equal health benefits for all.

6) The development of a society which encourages life-long critical evaluation of the ongoing social system.

7) The development of a society which encourages honest and open communication and which forces feelings of community and communion with others.

8) The development of a society which encourages creativity in all artistic areas.

9) The development of a society which is integrated at all levels, rather than compartmentalized.

10) The development of a society whose economic and

political system is not maintained at the expense or to the detriment of other people and nations.

We think about what we have learned from the activities we engaged in to break the coping pattern. Many communities are organized around exchanges of goods and services, cooperative store, collective decision making. We don't want to give up this power to control our own communities; our experience with economic and political democracy feels too good. Yet, there are 235 million of us, and we know that many of the products we stock our co-op stores with come from other parts of the country, and are made with raw materials not existing within the boundaries of our neighborhoods. While we want to maintain some degree of control over our lives, we realize that we are not self-sufficient and that we must depend on others for material and emotional support. Just as our Exchange has worked because people were willing to share, to see that their needs and interests could be better met if everyone's needs and interests were met at the same time, so too, the needs and interests of our community can best be satisfied by exchanging our services and products with those of other communities. We also realize that there are scarce natural resources and that for each of us to get a part of them, there must be some kind of national planning to insure an equal division based upon need. Yet, how can we have national planning at the same time as we have neighborhood and community decision making?

Suppose it were possible for each of us to have at our disposal, attached to our telephone, a computer hookup. Along with this computer hookup would be a directory which listed code numbers for all of the possible consumer goods we might want, as well as code numbers which could be used to communicate dissastisfaction we felt with the way in which our society was currently operating. Suppose, at the same time, we had a group of people similar to congresspersons, who would receive our communications, our votes on what we wanted produced, our grievances about the way our society was functioning. Yet, instead of receiving our opinions, and then making decisions for us, these "government officials" would receive the feedout from the centralized computer of all of our opinions, put these in the form of a bill, and then ask us to vote on what we wanted produced, again using our computer hookups for rapid decision making. Before we could be expected to make a decision, however, we would probably want to know certain facts. Does our nation have enough of the resources available to manufacture the commodity we desire? Can the product be manufactured without detriment to the environment, or to those engaged in its production? Are there other items having greater priority for which the natural resource which would go into the production of the goods we requested could be better put? Accordingly, we might want to have persons in our government who could help us answer these questions; experts who know what resources we had on hand, and understand the environmental impact of using these resources in a specific way.

What we are talking about, then, is designing a society in which we hold power, both in terms of what the society is to produce as well as in how the society is to satisfy its needs. Government would be a way of facilitating this process. Government facilitators, in fact, might be rotated every two years just to make sure more people had the opportunity to occupy these facilitative positions. But, who would produce the commodities we ordered? We would, at least some of them. Many of our most basic material needs could be met through automated plants, though we might decide that we would rather return to small-scale industries for the individualized production of such goods as shoes and other kinds of clothing. Since most of us will not be oriented toward owning superfluous consumer goods, only a few of us will have to be engaged in material production. But then, what will the rest of us do? We might stipulate that no one will have to work more than twenty hours a week, only we will no longer speak of work; rather, the type of contribution we will make to the community and society will be something we are deeply interested in. It will not be something that we must force ourselves to do. Extra effort will be made to automate all tasks no one wants to perform, or which people find distasteful or unchallenging. Since few of us are engaged in the production of material commodities, the rest of us would be pursuing artistic endeavors, exploring new ways of communicating, or making medical advances. Each of us, regardless of the twenty-hour contribution we made, would receive the same amount of "pay," except that our salary would be in the form of credit at a local market or consumer distribution center. Each of us would be allocated enough credit to satisfy our basic needs, and whatever credit we did not use each month would dissolve at the end of the month. Items we formerly had to save for —planes, houses, would be publicly owned. Anytime we wanted to use a boat, for example, we would simply sign up in much the same way as we currently register to stay at a state or national park. Homes would be leased for a year, with the possibility of yearly renewals.

The centralized computer then registers consumer need, and conveys this to district factories, where production is initiated, the workers at that plant deciding how the item is to be produced. After manufacture has been completed, the finished product is sent to distribution centers, where those who ordered the item can come pick it up. In the case of conflict between the use of a scarce resource for the production of two different items, the pros and cons of each would be figured out, and a bill submitted for a decision by the electorate. Everyone is eligible to vote, but only those persons can vote who first pass a voting test. The test would determine whether or not we understood the basic pro and con arguments entailed in production of a certain commodity. It would be the job of the government facilitators to supply information through news programs, newsletters, and other media of communication so that the public might become informed. Nor, having to work only twenty hours per week, would the devotion of a certain amount of time to becoming informed constitute a problem. Keeping up with what was going on, in fact, would be a part of our life-long educational commitment. Reading the newspaper would cease to be a chore, since we would be reading about our own activities and decisions.

Since most of our basic material needs might easily be satisfied, the issues we would primarily be expected to vote on would be concerned with quality of life —the need for a new hospital; foreign aid to a particular country; possible installation of a new mass transit system (since all but solar-powered cars would be outlawed).

Day-to-day problems we would need to deal with would, if possible, be resolved at the neighborhood or community level. Our educational system would be oriented along similar lines as the one we described in Chapter 14, that is, it would be problem-oriented. Neighborhood facilitators would be employed in cases where conflicts could not be settled amicably by the various parties involved in the dispute. When a problem arose, we would first ask if there was anything about the way our society was organized which might have caused the problem to occur (the crime, disease, sabotage of the national computer). If it was found that the community was deficient in some way, then a task force made up of community members would be assigned to clear up the problem. If the problem involved more than the community alone, it might be forwarded up to a regional or national council to facilitate resolution of the dispute. Such a council could then be charged with coming up with possible solutions, based on interviews with relevant constituencies, then presenting these solutions to a vote by the relevant population to decide which direction would be the most appropriate in which to proceed.

Educational institutions would not only teach students a curriculum based on problem-solving, but they would also acquaint them with various types of possible employment, especially in the arts and service areas where their talents might be most in demand. Critical evaluation of a wide variety of occupational experiences would prepare them to make a decision about what work they might like to engage in, as well as providing the opportunity to shift jobs at some future point should their chosen avocation prove no longer desirable. In fact, it might be expected that no one would stay in a particular occupation for more than a year or two, job rotation becoming the norm rather than the exception, as individuals solved problems they were interested in pursuing and then moved on to others. Moreover, workers would always be able to put in for educational leaves to retrain themselves in new occupations.

III

This alternative model of American society is based on the premise that everyone-wins, or everyone-loses. Power rests in the hands of the general population. There are no profits to be made, unless everyone profits. It has an economy geared toward a stable state; production being for the satisfaction of non-superfluous consumer needs. In this society insecurity is eliminated. We are not anxious as to where our next paycheck will come from, or whether or not we can out-compete our neighbor. We see the resolution of our problems as lying in the way in which our community is organized, and accordingly realize that our personal problems can only be effectively dealt with by working with others who help determine the scope of our dilemmas and what can be done about them. Our individualism is expressed through the contributions we make to the community and society and through the political decision-making power invested in us, rather than in the wardrobes we now adorn ourselves with, and the empty slogans of freedom and liberty we now shout under our breath as our manager tells us to work a little faster. It is a society which is in tune with the physical environment in which it resides, which produces goods which can be recycled or which are biodegradeable, and which takes into account the environmental impact of any political decision, just as individuals take into account the impact their actions will have on the community in which they live.

This may not be the alternative model of American society you would wish to live in. All well and good, for this society can be changed, just as we can mold the one we presently occupy to fit the needs of its inhabitants.

Acknowledgements

This essay owes a debt of gratitude to many social critics, whose work I have had the pleasure to read and ponder over the years. Among the most influential have been Herbert Marcuse, David Riesman, Saul Alinsky, Erich Fromm, Jonathan Kozol, Vance Packard, John Kenneth Galbraith, and Paul Goodman. A special thanks to Sid Tiedt for helping with designing an alternative elementary education curriculum.

I am also indebted to Cathy Herron for helping complete the finished manuscript.

— R.G.